WHAT I WISH I'D SAID

What I Wish I'd Said

AND OTHER THINGS THAT KEEP ME UP AT NIGHT

....

MARJIE ZACKS

What I Wish I'd Said: And Other Things that Keep Me Up at Night
Copyright © 2025 Marjie Zacks

No part of this publication may be reproduced or transmitted in any form or by any means, electronic or mechanical, including photocopying, recording or by any information storage and retrieval system, now known or to be invented, without permission in writing from the publisher.

Published by Marjie Zacks
Contact: mszacks53@gmail.com

ISBN: 978-1-7782553-4-2 (softcover)
ISBN: 978-1-7782553-5-9 (eBook)

Edited by Marial Shea
Cover and text design by: Jan Westendorp, Kato Design & Photo
eBook produced by Jan Westendorp, www.katodesignandphoto.com

Printed and bound in Canada

CONTENTS

Preface ix

When it's time to say nothing 1

Why do I say yes when I mean no? 3

The revenge of the pantyhose OR sometimes you really should say yes 6

No is a complete sentence OR guess who's coming to dinner? 10

When service disappoints OR profit vs overhead 13

My mom taught me 15

Biting my tongue 18

"Your wait time may be longer than usual" 21

Forgiving our own foibles 24

Is this seat taken? 26

Blue Lagoon, part 1: Cutting off my nose to spite my face 29

Blue Lagoon, part 2 31

Keeping cool under all kinds of pressure 34

Welcome to the Savoy . . . where worrying may be justified 37

Frank's prank OR not everyone shares the same sense of humour 42

Be careful what you wish for . . . you just might get it 46

How do you resist the urge to fix? 49

What does one say at a shiva or funeral? 52

When you miss your chance to say goodbye 54

The basement of so many memories 57

When I really should say "Yes!" 61

Letting go 64

The kinder may surprise you after all 67

The Bundt cake 70

Sniffing out the right nose 73

Starting off on the wrong foot 76

Speaking of friends we meet through our dogs 79

Meet my dog . . . and who are you, again? 82

Oh, to be young and driving the seniors home 86

Tongs very much 89

The self-phone generation 92

Did I really say that? 96

What goes around comes around 99

The real end of the story 101

The Good Samaritan 104

Better late than never 106

I wish . . . I could be good enough 109

A look on the bright side 113

Learning to say yes 116

When the rabbi calls 120

My Israeli family 123

The cane mutiny 127

Birds of a feather 132

An eye-opening visit 135

Everyone needs a Kitchen Cabinet 139

The family knish 142

Acknowledgements 145

About the Author 147

Preface

One of the frequent conundrums I face, apart from appearing older each time I look in the mirror, is whether or not all the things that happened over many years turned out the way I would have liked. I try not to spend a lot of time looking backwards because there is little to be done about past circumstances. But I want to make sure that when I do leave this earth (and I hope it is not for a good long time) I didn't repeat the same mistakes over and over again. Ideally, I should learn from my past so the future is easier and I don't spend my remaining years in the land of regret and recrimination.

What I Wish I'd Said is my third book. Part reflection on things past, it is also an opportunity to forgive myself, and perhaps others, while living in the present. Fittingly, as I write this, Yom Kippur, the Day of Atonement, is around the corner. Perhaps if I can understand my past foibles, they might teach me how to navigate the many challenges of the coming years as I age, hopefully gracefully.

Why didn't I say what I ended up wishing I had said? Was I too afraid to give voice to what I really thought? Was I so taken aback by what had transpired that I was too stunned to react in the moment? Why is it that, only after, while lying awake at night, I would think, "Oh, I wish I'd said this" or "I wish I'd said that."

And I'm not just talking about snappy comebacks. I also don't want to miss opportunities to express love or appreciation. The other day, for example, I remembered to acknowledge the city workers—the garbage guys, as I fondly call them. Week in, week out, they come by our house and deftly handle our refuse, dependably ridding us of what I can't dispose of anywhere, no matter how smelly and disgusting it is. A young man came this week in one of those new-fangled trucks that let him drive on either side, hop out, toss in the garbage and get back in faster than two people. He was so nice. When I handed him a box of chocolates for Christmas (and who knows what his holiday of choice is), he took off his glove, shook my hand as I stood there in my cheetah pajamas, and wished me a good Christmas. So polite. After hopping back in his truck, he came back and asked if he could put my bins up by my garage. I was dumbstruck! I just said "Thanks so much, but I've got them. Very nice of you though. Happy holidays."

I'm sharing these stories because I suspect I am not alone in pondering missed opportunities. Whether it is saying I'm sorry or expressing love and gratitude, or just standing up for my rights when someone treats me badly, the real trick is to "carpe diem"—to recognize the moment and seize the day. Maybe my efforts will bring you a laugh or a spark of recognition that will brighten your day. I sure hope so.

In short, this book is for all the people like me who have regrets over what they did not say at the time. I hope these stories make you feel less alone and inspire you to seize your moments and your days.

When it's time to say nothing

"Does this dress make my butt look fat?" How many spouses and partners have fallen into that trap? There is definitely a time to say nothing. Knowing when to keep shtum, as a friend of mine says, is an art. Lips tight together. Just think of when you've let something slip that should have stayed in your head. Suddenly everyone is looking at you, causing you to think, "Did I say that out loud"?

I'm still trying to figure out when to keep my mouth shut. As my husband says, there isn't a passerby or stranger I can't find common ground with and share a conversation about almost anything. I must have learned that from my years in public relations. But on the other hand, the older I get, the more opinionated I am, which can lead to an awkward moment or two. I really must remember, lips tight together! If no one asked me for my opinion, I'd best not give it.

We all treasure the friend who sighs in response to our troubles and with great empathy says, "uh-huh, uh-huh," metaphorically climbing down into the pit with us when we are down and sad. My temptation, however, is always to fix. What about this? What if you did that?

Shut up, Marjie. No one wants your input. They just want you to listen.

As the saying goes, "A wise man said...nothing." But how do you know when to say nothing? I'm often too busy putting my foot in my mouth to catch what's staring me in the face. Only afterwords do I remember that saying nothing is often best.

And what happens when you realize that those you love most have not learned the same lessons, and don't value the things you value? What happens when they don't see they have hurt you, or worse, they don't have the maturity to apologize in a meaningful way?

I'm going to keep shtum on those questions because I really don't know the answers. The longer I live, the more conundrums I find, and the more I see the value in keeping my mouth shut.

Why do I say yes when I mean no?

How often do we find ourselves saying yes when we really want to say no? Why, just today I said yes to a friend who needed a favour when I really wanted to say no. I think this has to do with how we were raised and whether we were taught that it's okay to say no. When I was growing up, I wouldn't have dreamed of saying no to my parents, or my teachers for that matter.

When I was in Grade 5, I found myself caught between a rock and a hard place. My parents had instructed me to bring home my books to do extra work over the Christmas holidays. Oh yeah, that was going to happen! My teacher, who we were all terrified of, told us, "No books are going home. You are to have a holiday." What to do? Argue with her? Or argue with my parents? Say yes to the old battle axe and no to my parents or yes to my parents and go head to head with every student's worst nightmare?

Somehow, I knew my parents would still love me. The Grade 5 teacher, on the other hand, would surely eat me. In the end, I made the right decision and left my books at school, though my parents were not amused and did not believe me when I told them we were not allowed to bring them home.

The ability to say no also depends on how conditioned you are to being a people pleaser. In my case, very. I think we can safely say that those, like me, who choose public relations for a career are natural people pleasers. We try to be liked and we help our client or organization be liked.

For me, pleasing others always seems to come before pleasing myself. Doing for others rather than pleasing myself was ingrained in me from childhood. I might never get the hang of saying no. No wonder I so often say yes grudgingly.

We have a gala to go to next weekend and I really want to say no to my husband. I don't like getting dressed up, I have yet to find shoes comfortable enough for standing around all evening with a glass of water in my hand, and I will know exactly two people at this affair, including me.

But then comes the guilt. What's my husband going to do, go alone? Not likely, and if he did, he would be put out. I begin to justify why I should say yes. "You might have a good time. You might meet new people. The keynote speaker may be good. The food might be yummy." I top this off with, "How bad can it be? Do it for your husband." And right there and then, I hear my mother saying, "Do it for me!"

My other trick to fool myself into doing something I don't want to do is to say to myself, "Self, on a scale of one to ten how bad do you think it will be?" And I answer, "Oh, about a seven?" And then when I get home from the dreaded event I ask, "So, how bad was it?" And I have to admit that it was really a three, so not that bad after all.

Why do we do this to ourselves? When do we realize we are old enough, experienced enough, with enough good judgment to take care of ourselves? Who needs high blood pressure? And therein lies the point. Self-care. I seem to put me on the list last. I'm sure I would be on the plane trying to hand out oxygen masks, then keeling over because I did not put mine on first.

But I am learning. And if a public relations professional trained from birth to say yes to everyone but herself can learn to say no, then there's still hope for all of us.

The revenge of the pantyhose OR sometimes you really should say yes

Putting on pantyhose, as dreadful as the invention is, was necessary for me to attend a dinner with my husband and 340 of my closest friends. "Come to a fundraiser for Israel at Chabad," my husband had encouraged. Having family in Israel, I didn't need much encouragement, I confess. After October 7th I had been making it my business to check in with my cousins there on a weekly basis.

"But do I have to wear a skirt?" My husband said he would check with a congregation member and report back. I didn't mind the skirt so much. What I was really asking was, "Will pantyhose be required?" Apparently, in the opinion of a longstanding member, they were. What I really wished was that I could wear pants. And what I wish in retrospect is that I had sprung for a new pair of pantyhose.

I have nothing against pantyhose. Thankfully, I was in the right lineup when they were giving out legs, so mine don't need to be hidden in pants. Other body parts haven't fared quite as well, but I digress.

So, there I was, trying to get the darn things on, my balance challenged by back, hip and knee issues. But for my husband, I was willing to make this concession, and heaven forfend I should offend anyone at the synagogue. Also, I had discovered that Chabad is a very kind, nonjudgmental organization. It felt home-like too, or *haymishe*, as they say in Yiddish, with kids running around and everyone warm and friendly. I never argued when it was time to show support for any initiative they held. The rabbi, a sweet and gentle man, had the good fortune to be married to a dynamo who knew how to organize, inspire and lead right alongside her husband of many years. She had been running the nursery school for ages. This event had her fingerprints all over it and it went off brilliantly, as usual.

Somewhere during the speeches and entertainment, I ducked out to visit the ladies' room, just to check on the pantyhose situation. Great, I thought, and forgot all about them. When I returned, Rabbi T, another black-hatted rabbi from the shul, was sitting in my seat visiting with our table and my husband. I like this man so much. He used to walk by our house on the way to synagogue on Friday evenings as we were sitting at the Shabbat dinner table with my family. He would spy my not-yet husband through the window and come in to say hello. The dog we had at the time did not like anyone in a black coat and he would go wild with barking. For Halloween, I made him go out in a black hat, *payos* (long sidelocks worn by very Orthodox men) and a black coat. When I told Rabbi T about this, he laughed and said, "*Baruch Hashem* (praise God). Bring him to *shul* (synagogue), we can use him for a *minyan* (gathering of ten men)." I told Rabbi T that we now have a girl dog. "She won't be much use for your minyan, but she's very sweet."

When Rabbi T realized he was sitting in my seat, he patted his knee and said, "Come sit here." Always with a fast comeback, I countered, "I will if you will," to which he smiled and responded, "Don't test me." I love this man. He's funny, witty and a joy to be with.

Before dinner, I had pointed out the rabbi to my husband, who reminded me, "No matter how much you like him, don't try to hug him. Don't touch him. Don't shake his hand, no matter what." Of course, I knew the rabbi was joking when he invited me to sit on his lap, as Chabad men do not touch women, and vice versa, unless they are married, and even then there are many rules. But I still wanted to hug him.

In the end, in spite of a delightful evening, it turned out that the pantyhose were no more enamored of me than I was of them. From being hauled out of a seldom-opened drawer where they had lived quite comfortably for at least twelve uninterrupted years, they were now plotting to get even on this wet and rainy night. But I didn't yet realize a revolution was underway. And I do mean under.

It was when I rose to get my coat from the cloak room that the fun began. My husband and I had taken separate cars, and I was leaving a bit early. I left the building, thanking the security guard who unlocked the gate to let me out onto the street. As I headed for my car, things started to slide, so to speak.

A police car was blocking the entrance but I was too distracted to notice anyone inside. My husband told me later that there was definitely an officer behind the wheel. Oh well. I must have provided him with entertainment as I struggled to try and pull up the revolutionaries that were going south along with the local geese.

Fortunately, I was wearing a skirt that was below the knee. Still, it was a crap shoot deciding whether to yank the damn things off altogether or hobble to my car with one hand on the umbrella and the other holding up what was left of the pantyhose. I decided to make a run for it. By the time I opened my car door, the pantyhose were around my ankles. Giving them a final tug, I drove home, where I promptly ripped them off and threw them in the garbage.

Up until that point it had been a lovely evening. In hindsight did I wish I'd said no? Absolutely not. I was glad we went. I wouldn't have missed kibbitzing with my favourite rabbi for anything in the world, pantyhose notwithstanding!

I have no idea what I will do in February for a neighbour's wedding we're invited to. Maybe it's time to buy a new pair of pantyhose in a larger size. Or maybe I will buy a long dress that goes to the floor. Stay tuned.

No is a complete sentence OR guess who's coming to dinner?

Seems I am not the only one who wishes they had said what they were thinking at the time. In chatting with friends, I've discovered that they too wish they'd had the courage to speak up on many occasions. For example, my neighbour James was telling me about his New Year's Eve. James is a dab hand at smoking. No, not funny things, although I can't swear to that. I mean he has a smoker in his backyard, and during the pandemic he started a small business selling smoked briskets. Why not? Eating was the one thing we could all safely do at that time. His business took off. Occasionally, he would bring us a sample of what he was cooking.

For New Year's Eve he invited all his wife's friends for dinner. He told them that the main courses were looked after and asked them to bring something as a starter or side dish, a dessert and whatever they wanted to drink. How lucky to get an invite when they weren't even his own friends? Nice guy.

The day after New Year's, my husband and I bumped into him when we were out walking our dogs, who are good friends. (Appropriately, James's dog is named Beefie.) When I wished

James a happy new year, my husband and I watched as his face turned into the biggest scowl. He said, "Let me tell you about my New Year's Eve.

"I bought a $500 roast of wagyu beef and all I asked was that the guests bring something. One offered coleslaw, which I did not need, but okay. Another, when asked to bring veggies and dip said she would bring the dip, but someone else could bring the veggies."

"Really?" I asked.

"Really," he replied. "Not only that, one woman actually asked if she could bring her grown son as he liked smoked beef. He's mid-twenties and six-foot four. This guy could eat us out of house and home. Next thing I know, my wife is pulling out turkey from the freezer in case we run out of food."

As he shook his head, I asked him why he couldn't say, "Maybe next time. This is just for my wife's friends—you know, our generation. The only kids there will be mine as they live here." Or "I appreciate that you might not want to leave him alone on New Year's Eve but this is just for us older adults. Another time."

He glared at me and said, "Man I wish I could have!"

Well, why not? If someone is asking for something they have no business asking, why can't we say no? It's not like this son couldn't be left alone. He was a grown man, for heaven's sake! And yet we don't speak up. I have yet to figure out why it is easier to stew and complain after the fact than to find the courage we need in the moment.

Another friend of mine wanted a quiet dinner for six but then felt she must include a relative who wanted to bring her kids along—kids in their late teens, early twenties! Is it me or is this chutzpah, a brazen act, and an inconsiderate one at that?

Why can't we say no?

At lunch with my friend Brenda, we were discussing our inability to speak our truth in a nice but assertive manner. She told me that she had made a lovely dinner for a couple who were her husband, Todd's, friends. Dinner was ready, but they were late. The phone rang and they announced that friends of theirs (with their two kids) whom they hadn't seen in ages just happened to drop in, and could they bring them to dinner too?

Are you kidding me? Who does that? Good for Brenda. She screwed up her courage and calmly spoke her truth. "I'm sorry," she said, "but there isn't enough food for four more people." What a great answer, although in our household there would probably be enough left over for an army, so I would never think to say it.

Someone please tell me when it is okay to say, "No way. Not tonight. Another time," without all the accompanying guilt. Why do we have to worry about someone else's fragile feelings when no one worries about ours? Why can't we bring ourselves to say what we really feel when someone else clearly has no couth? Maybe we fear that we would end up with no one at our dinner table at all. It is a mystery for sure.

The rude "friends," with their four unexpected guests, decided not to come after all, so Brenda and Todd had dinner by themselves. I never asked if the friendship survived.

When service disappoints OR profit vs overhead

I used to go to a nearby coffee shop that had become a hangout for the local high school kids. (Where do they get the money for overpriced coffee?) One day, after placing my order, I looked around for an empty table. There were many, as the school lunch rush was over, but they were all covered in crumbs and spills.

When I asked one of the young women at the counter if I could have a napkin or something to wipe off a table, she seemed nonplussed. After thinking for a moment, she handed me a wet cloth. I was too amazed to respond. Did it occur to her as I was wiping down table and chairs that this was actually part of her job? When I went back and asked for something to dry the table, again I was met with the dazed look. I got to thinking, Why are some people motivated while others are just putting in time, or, as they say now, phoning it in?

One of our last remaining Canadian department stores provided me with an excellent opportunity to bite my tongue. I was at the counter trying to buy twenty-two pairs of Olympic souvenir mittens for the volunteers who had worked with me on an international project. I waited and waited as three staff discussed hair, nails and their dates from the night before. After a good five minutes, I asked if it was possible to pay or would they please get their manager if they were too busy. Suddenly I got served. I kept my cool and my mouth shut, but I couldn't help thinking, "Hey guys, wake up. I am profit. You are overhead."

Allow me one final story. Friends of mine took their grandkids bowling. In the next lane, kids were climbing all over the place, taking the balls meant for my friends and their grandkids and slipping and sliding down the greased surface of other bowlers' lanes. The grandparents had a hard time hanging onto their tempers, but no one from the bowling alley said a word. Keep in mind that an afternoon of frivolous fun at the bowling alley is no longer an inexpensive proposition. The bill for the lanes and the shoes and the balls, and whatever all else, came to eighty dollars.

Fortunately, this story has a happy ending. My friends emailed the bowling alley asking why staff had not tried to provide a safe, enjoyable experience. Days went by with no response, so they sent another message with the heading "Second email on this matter." This time the owner of the bowling alley responded with a phone call. She apologized for not seeing the first email, gave my friends a complete refund for their ruined afternoon and invited them back for a do-over on the house.

That's not just good business sense. The manager took responsibility, accepted the blame and made good to refund their customer's money. Though this story ended well, getting that positive response took perseverance, patience, determination—and speaking up in the right tone at the right time using the right means of communication after finding the right person. It sure worked for my friend and her family.

My mom taught me

Let me tell you about a wonderful late-thirties server who came to our restaurant table and introduced himself: "Hello, I'm Darren."

Darren had started at that restaurant just two weeks before, and from what I could see, he was a great hire. He was super interested, very chatty, gave us great eye contact, and actually seemed to care about us. He asked about allergies and made sure the ones I mentioned were not an issue with what I had ordered. He timed how our food came out and chatted with us in between courses. He was marvelous.

Honestly, I think Darren should be training all the other service workers in existence on how to make the customer the focus. Someone taught him how to be a *mensch* (a good human being). I wondered who should get the credit, and then made sure *I* gave him the credit he deserved by leaving him a generous tip and, later, calling his boss to tell him what a good hire Darren was.

Another day, while my dog was at the groomer, I found a coffee shop where I could wait. After a recent disastrous visit to a premier (meaning expensive) international coffee emporium, I decided to stick to my Canadian roots. At least this place knew how to top up my decaf with a third of a cup of hot chocolate, which for me makes coffee drinking so much better.

So there I sat, savouring a little peace and quiet and reading my novel, when in came a gaggle of students on their lunch break. Ah, the exuberance of youth—chatting loudly with expletives slipping from their lips every few words. Some wore earbuds, oblivious of their over-loud voices. This is usually my cue to make my exit, but I was well into my book, minding my own business.

I was aware that Granny Grey Hair had sat down two tables over. (I call her that with great affection, first because she looked like everyone's favourite granny, and second, with due respect, as I have yet to let my true colours out since going grey at about age thirty.) She had her cell phone on the table along with a coffee and pastry.

Three high school students arrived, young men in their mid-teens. Two of them loped off to the counter to order. The third approached Granny Grey Hair and said, "Good morning. How are you today?" The poor woman looked bafflegabbed. What on earth? The young man proceeded to ask if she minded if he and his friends sat in the corner next to her table, or would that be crowding her?

Now I was interested. What was this, a young human being with manners? How marvelous. Granny said it would be fine for them to sit there. As she started sliding her chair closer to me to make room, our eyes met, wide with surprise, as if to say, "Did I dream it or is this kid really polite?" I looked right back at her and said, "How do you like that? You don't see that very often."

She remarked that young folk often come in and immediately start swearing and "behaving like animals."

I felt our polite young man was owed a compliment and said to him, "Wow, somebody raised you right!" He immediately responded, "My mom taught me." And didn't she do a marvelous job? How delightful. I was so happy that someone took the time to teach their offspring how to be a mensch.

On my way out to pick up my dog, I could not resist adding, "Tell your mom that a complete stranger told you what a good job she did raising you."

It sure is nice to know that some of those inheriting our crazy, mixed-up world will be able to handle it.

Biting my tongue

The invitation said 4:30 p.m. At 4:00 p.m. we pulled out of our driveway for what we thought would be a ten-minute drive. Pedal to the metal, we made it on time. But where were all the guests? Seems there had been a bad accident on a major highway and many guests were delayed.

I guess no one told the rabbi, who was pacing under the chuppa. We sat quietly in our masks, having just gotten over Covid a few weeks prior and not wanting to repeat the experience any time soon. This was a fancy occasion. Formal wear, the invite had said. We enjoyed our own company as we marveled at the sixty- and seventy-year-olds in dresses so short they required workout shorts underneath. The make-up! The five-inch spiked golden glitter shoes with a large butterfly on each back. The one-piece leather jumpsuit that one of my arms might have fit into. People love to get dressed up, but really, some seemed over the top. I was clearly getting old.

Finally, the ceremony was underway. Lovely. Then the traditional cocktail hour with hors d'oeuvres, which never fail to remind me of something uttered many years ago (forty-four years, to be precise, back when I was working in the hotel industry) by an American colleague not familiar with the French language. She was reviewing wedding festivities with a mother of the bride and said, "And then there will be time for Horas Davorahs!" At first, I had no idea what she was saying, then I burst out laughing. Hors d'oeuvres were never the same after that. Funny how some things stick with you through the years.

On to the dinner and getting some two hundred hungry attendees seated at their correct tables. The bride and groom were introduced, followed by a few opening remarks. Or at least I think that's what happened. I couldn't really hear. Only as the evening wore on did I realize we could not hear because of the table of ten beside us. They were having a grand old time laughing and carrying on. They never did come up for air, not even during the speeches, which happened to be worth listening to.

Here we are again: I could have said something. I wanted to say something. Why didn't I say something?

I was on my way to tell them a thing or two when my husband firmly pulled me back into my place, saying, "You don't know them, it's not your business and don't bother, as they will probably just give you a piece of their minds." So I just sat there and stewed quietly.

Finally, when I got up to go to the ladies' room, I could see that my husband was panicking. I assured him I had no intention of speaking to the guests at the noisy table. I pointed to the woman on my left, whose company I had enjoyed all evening, and said, "She's going to do it for me!"

At that, they both broke up laughing, and our shared frustration and tension dissolved.

I've said it before and I'll say it again (and I hope I'm listening): We have to learn to speak up, but we also have to know when to keep quiet. All those folks at that noisy table were wedding guests, just like us. We were all invited. This was not my wedding.

And anyway, the merriment on the dance floor turned out to be way more fun than disapproving of my fellow revelers.

"Your wait time may be longer than usual"

It started at nine o'clock on a January morning, with a poor, sad raccoon sitting in the freezing cold trying to get closer to the warmth from a house down the street. The sun was actually shining, even if the temperature was around zero. No self-respecting, sane raccoon should be about in the daylight, as every barking dog passing by knew. I couldn't understand until my friend and I, along with my trusty wheaten terrier, approached the house where said raccoon was resting. My dog immediately went berserk. A raccoon to a terrier is tantamount to waving the proverbial red flag in front of a bull. My dog is a rodent getter, a raccoon her favorite challenge.

Trying to find an animal rescue service is hard at the best of times, but even more of a challenge since our city took over the task, then gave it to the SPCA, then took it back, then farmed it out to another agency. Animal rescue now seems about as approachable as a raccoon sitting on one's driveway in broad daylight.

Nevertheless, I tried. I called in about the racoon, but was told the number was changed and to dial 211 and the city would handle it. That is when I heard the message, "We are currently experiencing high call volume," blah blah blah, "but if you leave your number, we will call you back."

Two hours later, as I was driving out of town to visit another friend, I still had not heard from the city. The raccoon could have been halfway to Las Vegas by then, but he did look rather sad and sick, so maybe he was right where I left him. I moved on to Plan B.

Plan B was my friend Kayla, whom I had nicknamed "Neighbourhood Watch." She is the best kind of friend: kind, caring, an excellent listener, and she always remembers the last story you told her. She's also the best next-door neighbour, the responsible one who organizes a committee if there are too many tenants living in the house down the street dealing drugs at all hours of the night. She will go to bat for you and not quit until she has succeeded.

I called Kayla and told her about the racoon, and she said she would try to help. Sure enough, within ten minutes she had found the correct phone number, and the rescue people were on their way.

This is the best kind of friend to have. The one who you know will always get the job done. You know what they say: Want to get it done? Give it to a busy person. Why are they always so busy? Because they actually take pride in a job well done and won't rest until it is done and done right.

I'm off to walk my dog now and to check that there are no other raccoons who need rescuing. Hopefully it will be a quiet day. I'm certainly able to call the next time I see a raccoon out in broad daylight. I just wish I knew who to call at the city offices. If only they didn't keep changing who is responsible. When I worked for a national charity, I loved being on calls with our Quebec team, especially the way they would ask, "Who is the responsible?" It flows better in French, but you get the idea.

Forgiving our own foibles

Anyone can make a mistake. I know. I have had a hell of a week. Monday was particularly bad. My father-in-law was in the hospital. It was a hugely stressful time for the whole family. We were trying to keep an eye on his aging wife, who was missing her husband terribly.

Also on Monday, it was my turn to book the golf tee-off time for my women's league. If you don't call precisely at a ridiculous hour on a Monday evening, good luck getting a time to play the following week. All day long, as I did my errands and chores (so badly they needed redoing), I kept reminding myself, "Don't forget to call for the tee time." Nevertheless, it was nearly bedtime, long after the booking time, when I realized I had completely forgotten and now three other women were going to be as mad at me as I was at myself. I tried in vain to call late and get a time, but there were none left.

In the grand scheme of things how important was this? Well, the booking was my turn and I didn't want to let anyone down. It never occurred to me to hand off the task to one of the other golfers whose lives might have been somewhat less chaotic than mine was on that particular day. All night I tossed and turned. Oh, why did I screw up?

I made sure to phone the pro shop right when it opened the next morning, at 6:30. I was so blurry-headed from lack of sleep and worry that I couldn't even punch in the numbers correctly. No answer. Fortunately, I finally connected with someone who seemed totally unaware of my angst and calmly gave me a pretty good tee time. As I called my colleagues to let them know, they each told me they might not make it after all. One had an appointment. Another had a reunion lunch.

Later that week, I received a call from a charity I support. Seemed I'd filled in the form that same Monday, giving them my credit card information, but neglecting to tell them how much I was donating. After telling the woman I was grateful she had not charged my card and left for Europe with the funds, I provided the financial information. I was really on a roll that day.

Here's my point: We are all human. We are all doing the best we can. Forgiving ourselves for our own foibles is just as important, if not more so, as forgiving others for theirs. Some days are just better than others, for everyone, and it's important to remember we are all human. It's okay to ask for help. It's okay to acknowledge we are having a bad day, week, month, year. I doubt there is anyone alive today who would not empathize. Life is just like that.

Next time I will ask someone else to take over the task that is one too many. What's so bad about that? And who knows, the person who says yes may have been waiting all day for a chance to help.

Is this seat taken?

When I booked seats for my husband and me for a long flight, I had a strategy. I booked us each an aisle seat across from each other so I could get up and walk around without bothering anyone. Little did I realize this meant that others would be climbing over us.

My husband's strategy, on the other hand, was to book an aisle seat and the seat next to it. That way, there would be only one person climbing over us from the window or in the middle section of the plane—possibly no one if the other two seats were occupied by a couple. Besides, we could lean against each other. But by the time he shared his superior strategy, the flight was full so I was unable to change the seats.

Okay, then, we decided to combine our strategies and play it by ear. We would prevail upon the kindness of others to switch with us once on board.

When we boarded, however, someone was sitting in my aisle seat—a portly man with his wife across from him in her own aisle seat. I guess they thought they could have the entire row. So much for my plan.

I politely said, "Excuse me, I believe this is my seat." His wife began to grouse loudly, explaining in her language that her husband was not to move over under any circumstances. What to do? This was my seat. I didn't want to start a war, but I also didn't want the middle seat for an eleven-hour flight. The man eventually realized he had no choice and moved to his seat. His wife, meanwhile, buzzed for an attendant.

While this was going on, an even larger, taller woman was arriving to take the middle seat next to my husband. I slyly asked if she would like an aisle seat, and she quickly thanked me and switched without realizing that the large man was now in the middle, beside her.

Happily for us, my husband now took the middle seat in his row, with me next to him, which was what he'd wanted all along, and I had the aisle seat, which was what I wanted, leaving the others in their row to battle it out for themselves. You could hear the yelling and ruckus caused by the husband and wife all the way to the back of the plane, where the attendant did manage to find them a row all to themselves. Whew.

I was telling this story of airplane musical chairs to a fellow traveler. In return, she told me about booking aisle seats for herself and her husband months ahead for a flight where there were eight seats in the middle row. Once aboard, a mother with many children and other family members insisted that the couple move to non-aisle seats so she could keep her family together. My traveler friend calmly replied, "No. I specifically chose these seats and I will not move." The mom was irate, and her kids climbed all over the place throughout the flight.

What a novel idea, saying what we really mean to say and standing our ground (or air, in this case). Our friend wondered, all these years later, why she even had to think twice about claiming the seats she had booked in advance and paid for.

Like many women, I tend to be accommodating, wanting to keep the peace. However, we must stand up (or sit down) for our rights and occupy the seat we booked and paid for. "Sorry, no can do," is the obvious response, with no guilt. In the words of child-raising guru Barbara Coloroso, we need to, "Say what we mean, mean what we say and do what we said we were going to do." Thank you for moving. This is my seat!

Blue Lagoon, part 1:
Cutting off my nose to spite my face

When my daughter was ten years old, and I was a single parent, we took a wonderful trip to Australia to visit family. What I didn't do on that trip that we were supposed to do was visit the Blue Lagoon in Fiji. Friends of ours had done this trip with their daughter. In fact, I'm sure there aren't too many places in the world the three of them had not visited, such was their opportunity to travel over school vacations, as both parents were teachers. And, oh, how they prepared for each trip. There was no internet in those days; instead, they read up on their destinations in encyclopedias and dutifully took out the relevant library books so they were all well briefed by the time they reached their vacation spot.

I, on the other hand, was somewhat less prepared. But with my daughter, I knew the itinerary had to have an element of spontaneity, spur of the moment "Let's do that"—at least, to the degree you can do that on a trip to the other side of the world, where the water in the toilet really does spin the other way and the light is really unlike anything I had experienced in our hometown in Canada. I tried to be spontaneous. However, the Blue Lagoon cruises fill up months, if not years, in advance.

When our friends went on this very cruise, they were told children travel free. What the brochure did not say is that if you are a single parent, too bad, your child is now considered a spouse at full fare. There was no "kids go free" unless there were two parents. I felt that was not only bad representation, but poor practice, and I wanted desperately to argue with someone about the unfairness of the policy. Try as I might, I could not get them to see my point of view, so I decided I would not go on the cruise. I actually said what I wanted to say and it didn't make one darn bit of difference. Their policy was not changing, and I was not coming down off my high horse, so we were not going on the Blue Lagoon cruise. As my mother would say, "Nothing like cutting off your nose to spite your face."

Over the years I followed what was going on in Fiji, and learned there was a civil war at the time that made Fiji impossible to visit. Then life just got too hectic. Time passed and so did the opportunities for travel to this island destination. Then, some thirty years later, I was scheduled to go on a Habitat for Humanity build to, of all places, Fiji. How exciting to finally get there! Maybe I could do the Blue Lagoon cruise after all.

It was not to be. Covid arrived and all plans to go anywhere quickly evaporated. My husband, wanting to console me, said, "Never mind, I will take you to Fiji some day." Thrilled with the prospect, I made our plans. However, Covid stuck around and stuck around and, finally, after postponing the trip several times, three years later we were set to leave.

Blue Lagoon, part 2

Having chosen not to take my ten-year-old daughter on the Blue Lagoon cruise on principle, I regretted the decision for many years.

Funny how time fixes many things. Decades later, when I took this trip at last, this time with my husband, I realized that the cruise was not for children after all. Instead, we were joined by about twenty-five sixty-something-year-olds, one family of four, and one or two other couples. Not a child to be found. I could see how a youngster would be totally out of place—not just inappropriate, but probably miserable. It was nice to know I had made the right decision, even if it had been for the wrong reason.

Every day our traveling hotel (aka catamaran) would tie up to a palm tree on a small island. We could swim ashore or take a tender (small boat). The catamaran was so close to shore that the cruise director could hold aqua aerobics off the back deck while we all bobbed in the shallow water. Lunch and a portable bar were transported to wherever we happened to anchor that day.

The family with the two twenty-something sons was remarkable, though not because the two boys were the youngest on board with all us older codgers. It was because they truly seemed to be having a wonderful time partying together and drinking up a storm. The mom would hang in with them for so long, then go read a book in peace and quiet, but the dad was having as much fun as the sons; in fact, they acted like playmates. I watched as the older brother snuck up on the younger just as he finally managed to get onto a paddle board, giving it a huge shove from behind, toppling his sibling head first into the Blue Lagoon. He and his dad laughed and laughed. I watched on the catamaran's "disco night" as the mom and boys all got up to line dance in perfect sync with each other. Clearly this was not a one-off.

Wow. Kids and parents, having a great time together. I was so envious. Though the boys were in the room next to us, we never heard a peep from them as they slept off the vast quantities of alcohol they had consumed. The next day, the family was back at it, sitting in the tiny pool on the back deck with drinks in hand, not a care in the world. The dad didn't even shave during the entire cruise and was obviously having the time of his life.

I overheard the mom tell another traveler that she was an emergency response nurse at a busy hospital in Sydney, Australia. What the other three did I would find out only when we got chatting on the last night of the cruise. Seems the boys were on holiday from work. Of course, I had to ask where they worked, and they replied, "in the court system." That made me even more curious, so I asked how it was that they both worked there. Were they lawyers? No, they told me, they were clerks, but their dad worked in the legal system. When asked if he may have had a hand in getting them work in the courts, they sheepishly said yes. When I asked the next obvious question, "So is your dad a lawyer?" they became even more sheepish.

Turns out their dad was a Criminal Court Justice. I was blown away. Just goes to show you can never judge a book by its cover. That unshaven, hard-partying guy might turn out to be a judge on vacation to let his hair down. Even more remarkable to me was the family's closeness. That bond they shared with one another was enough to make any family envious.

As we doddering seniors climbed in and out of tenders to be motored to shore and hang out under the palm trees, I was very glad this trip was shared with my husband and not a young child. We snorkeled and swam, sailed, and had tea and dinner with the locals. Though my husband and I had a somewhat less inebriated holiday than the family of four, we enjoyed it just as much. But clearly, the cruise was no place for a ten year old. I could finally let that regret go. Some things can only be appreciated when you are older. It was the trip of a lifetime, for sure.

Keeping cool under all kinds of pressure

I had a special birthday coming up, so I was off on a trip to celebrate. Navigating through the airport at 7 a.m. is always a challenge. Long lineups. New technology. Ever-changing rules about what you can carry on in your luggage and what you can't. Arrival and check in, security and all of the airport routine went smoothly. Now I had time to just sit, have breakfast and relax.

About twenty-five minutes before boarding, I suddenly realized I wasn't sure where my iPad was. I knew I'd packed it, and I knew I took it out going through security, but I had no recollection of seeing it in the bin and putting it back in my bag. Just to be sure, I opened my carryon to check. It was not there.

Oh, no. Instant hot flash. Suddenly, my perfectly comfortable sweatshirt felt like a winter coat in summer. I was soaking. Ah, the joys of getting older.

I ran to the nearest agent to find out if they could call up to security. "No, we don't do that," I was told.

"Well, how do I find my iPad that I left there?"

"You have to go to Arrivals and go through the process of Customs as if you just landed here."

You have got to be kidding me.

Trying to be helpful, the agent said, "I can let you through the door." Except that put me in the connecting flight line. "No," they said. "You have to go to Arrivals. You are not connecting from one flight to another."

The sweat was now gathering in full force. I could feel it trickling down my back, through my hairline and down my face. So much for having my hair done the day before, and putting makeup on, which I rarely do. Now I was just a puddle.

Grabbing my bag, I ran to Arrivals, checked back in to my country (which I had never left), explained the forgotten iPad and fast-hoofed it back up four floors to Departures to start all over again. When I finally got to Security, one of the guards recognized me. "Didn't I just see you this morning?" Observant and smart! I wouldn't have recognized the dishrag of a sweaty human I had become. I explained my issue and he let me in and even wished me good luck.

Now, where was that iPad? It's amazing how attached I'd gotten to a five-by-seven piece of technology. No one had seen it. The guard at the desk was kind enough to give me his personal phone number and said to call him later if I hadn't heard from him. If the iPad hadn't shown up by the time I came back home on Sunday, I could check lost and found.

I just wanted to get on a plane. Now all this hassle.

Suddenly, I had a thought. Maybe I should check my bag one more time. Right there in the lineup, I dropped to my knees, opened my bag and noticed the zippered inside pocket. I never put anything in there in case it bulges past the allowable size. But why was the zipper open?

Lo and behold, there was my iPad. No wonder no one could see it at security or on the camera footage. Some kind soul on the security line decided to put it back in my bag for me. Now I felt completely foolish. I quickly called back to my security buddy and told him I had it and thanked him for his unnecessary concern.

By the time my boarding section was called, I was so obviously flustered that the agent didn't even suggest I check my bag. Now I had five hours to sit in my seat, dry out and try to relax. It was going to be a good trip after all.

Welcome to the Savoy...
where worrying may be justified

The smile that greeted us was the most striking first impression. It had no front teeth. Strange for a front desk manager of what was once a luxury hotel with a solid international reputation. That was our introduction to our hotel in Rome.

We had spent a few days in Florence followed by a few more in Venice, where, sadly, the porters and gondoliers were holding one of their frequent strikes, which also affected the railways, making getting to one's hotel a challenge. Dragging our luggage up and down the many stairs and bridges while walking across the numerous cobblestoned squares and piazzas was our introduction to that famed city. Also, we noted that if you purchased any gemstones or jewelry at the Murano glass factory they escorted you back to your hotel where they had picked you up. If you did not make a purchase, and we had not, you were escorted out the back door, greeted by an empty canal and the challenge of finding your own way home. How does one hail a gondolier, anyway?

When we arrived in Rome, we spent the day touring marvels of one of the world's most popular cities. Yes, it was crowded, but there was something about visiting the Colosseum, with its ancient history that let you imagine the roar of the crowds as the gladiators battled it out with the lions so many years ago. There's a story told about public speaking, said to be the number one fear of most humans. It tells of a lion who refused to eat the gladiator once he had him cornered. Turns out someone had whispered in his ear that after dinner he would be required to speak. That turned his stomach enough to reject the human meal.

After a day of touring the Arch of Titus and the Roman Forum, where the chariots raced during the time of Cleopatra, and after ambling down the famed Via Veneto with its exquisite shops and sixteen lanes for cars (or so it seemed, not that the drivers in Rome stick to any one lane), we headed to our hotel for check-in. That was when the adventure began.

Despite my muttered misgivings to my husband, who is a very forgiving kind of guy and saw nothing unusual in the front desk manager missing his front teeth, we completed the paperwork and were shown to our fourth-floor room. It was old but nicely furnished in an antique sort of vibe. Because it started to teem buckets of rain and the hotel was out of umbrellas, we had dinner in the covered rooftop restaurant. Nice menu, good food. All was fine.

Apparently, while we were soundly sleeping that night after our day of travel and touring, there was a power failure. The next morning, we heard about it at breakfast in the basement of the hotel from guests who had been caught taking a shower when the power went out and had to rinse off by the light of their iPads. (This was 2011, and we did not yet own iPads, so it was a bit of a stretch to understand how they worked as a light for the shower.)

On day two, I thought it odd that the elevator was out of service and even odder that the computers were down. However, after taking in many sights, including the Spanish Steps and Trevi Fountain, we fell into bed not overly concerned. Around three in the morning, I awoke thinking someone had knocked on our door. As I came fully awake, I heard knocks on all the other doors down the hall. While my husband slept, I poked my head out into the hallway. Our neighbour was also looking out to see who had knocked. I asked her if she thought this was a case of Nicky Nicky Nine Doors. She shrugged. Then I heard a faint fire alarm that did not quite reach to our floor, perhaps explaining the door knocking. And then I could hear the distant sirens of fire trucks coming closer.

This was not a drill.

Realizing there was a fire somewhere in the building, I put my best crisis management skills into action. I gathered what I thought were the most important items, in this order: hair dryer, cameras, passports, wallets, a change of clothes for us both. Only then did I wake my husband to let him know he had about three minutes to dress and get out of there. We tumbled down the hotel stairs to the lobby, where everyone was gathering. What were they doing standing there in their pajamas? Get out! Quick! Meanwhile, the front desk manager was desperately calling to reach the general manager, who had locked the front doors and gone home. No keys. Not a good situation.

The general manager finally arrived, or the firemen did, and let us out.

As I headed down the street, I explained to my husband that we were not going back there. So began our search for another hotel.

When we came back at 5:30 a.m., we were told there had been a small fire in the computer room (yah, right). We had pre-paid for our rooms online, so I marched up to the desk and asked for our money back: the entire amount for all nights booked. Eventually, the general manager agreed and we moved to the new hotel, a major chain that actually lived up to its reputation. Okay, so the cost for one night was what we would have paid for two at the original hotel, but with a refund for four nights and only two left in Rome, we broke even.

Never mind that the concierge at the new hotel was snooty and intimidating, causing us to slink by him every time we entered the hotel. "I am an ex-hotel person," I wanted to say. "I worked for years in the industry. Don't be snooty to me. You are a doorman. I was management!" He made me wish I had brought my finest ballroom attire just to walk into the lobby. He tried to get us a taxi to go a very short distance, and when we thanked him but said we would walk, he turned up his nose and moved on to other guests. Well, at least he had his front teeth.

Back home, my husband insisted I write my usual review of our stay in that first hotel in Rome. Even though I had very good reason, I never sent in a survey or letter. I must have gotten too busy with work, so I never said what I really thought, which was that someone was not minding the store. For a hotel chain of that size and reputation, I wondered if they ever refurbished the tired décor. They definitely needed to spruce up the place.

As reviews go, I could have really gotten my teeth into that one.

Frank's prank OR not everyone shares the same sense of humour

The bus pulled away with Frank at the microphone. He immediately laid out the rules. No arriving late. On board by 6:30 a.m. No tardiness getting back on the bus after a lunch or touring stop. Then he launched into the history of the country we had just arrived in. With its beauty and tragedy, its history of conflict and adversity, we were about to discover all of the magnificence (natural) and devastation (man-made) of South Africa.

We had discovered a fairly reasonable tour company out of New York. After an eighteen-hour flight, with a stopover in Johannesburg on our way to Cape Town, the tour's starting point, we were exhausted. As the bus rode along, we were introduced to our fellow travelers, mostly American, and the breathtaking scenery.

Table Mountain, our first stop, was truly something to behold. A cable-car ride up to the top gave us a view of the waves crashing below on one side of the flat-topped natural wonder and the city spread out beneath a rising sun on the other. We were excited to be on this adventure.

Little did we know that our tour guide was on the last or second-to-last tour of his career after doing this work for the better part of his adult life. He had also done a stint in the Israeli army, but clammed up immediately if we showed any interest in this part of his personal history. He did, however, tell us he was Afrikaner and spoke the language. His family had been landowners in the Transvaal and he grew up during the Apartheid years. As a result, he was well versed in the history of this part of Africa.

On the day we were to tour Cape Town, the city was congested with a parade as the prime minister and his three wives marched on foot to the parliament buildings, followed by a procession of cars and party members on foot. Frank was somewhat annoyed that he couldn't take us on the scheduled tour of the city. Therefore, we ended up going to the Garden Synagogue, with its wonderful museum. We were quite delighted with the turn of events.

I was able to look up information on my Cape Town relatives and trace their arrival by ship from Europe some ninety years earlier. As listed on the ship's manifest, mine was a family of cabinetmakers, which seemed about right, as my zaide in Massachusetts was a carpenter and head of the union. In the manifest listings I found the names of all the children who came with their parents, and those who settled in Cape Town. I learned that my family actually wanted to continue on to North America to meet up with the rest of the family who left Europe before the Holocaust. However, they were told that it would cost them more, so they disembarked to make enough money to continue the journey. It was unclear to me whether they remained there due to a lack of funds or whether this was the era when Jews were not allowed into the United States or Canada.

We had a marvelous time on the trip. Made some lifelong friends from Massachusetts. They had forgotten their alarm clock so asked me if I would call to wake them up each morning. To do that I would need their room number. Problem was, every time we checked in to a hotel and got settled, there they would be, trudging down the hall with their luggage. "What happened?" we would ask. "Oh, the toilet didn't flush." "The phone didn't work." "We were right beside the elevator." So it was that every night at dinner in a new hotel I would have to ask, "Which room did you end up in? Are you sure? Is this where I call in the morning?" Frank was not amused. In fact, Sarah and Bert quickly became his least favourite travelers, as he had to arrange a change of rooms each time they were not satisfied.

At one stop Frank admonished us, "Be back on the bus in one hour. If you are not here I am leaving without you." True to his word, when one younger tour member was not on the bus on time, Frank told the driver to pull the bus forward when he saw her approaching in the rearview mirror. Then Frank told him to stop, let her catch up, then drive off again. This went on for a few stops and starts. Frank was killing himself laughing, and then we were all laughing, along with the late arrival. She was young enough to run after the bus each time.

But if he had pulled that on me, I might have had a few choice words.

So Frank had a mischievous streak. Who knew? He was also a walking archive of facts, figures, historical events and knowledge, a wealth of which he shared with us every day on the bus as we traveled from one part of the country to another. Only thing was, we were exhausted from the pace. On one day-long trip from one city to another, I dozed off. Sometime later, I asked Frank a question, to which he responded, "Well, if you hadn't fallen asleep during my talk you would know the answer," and haughtily stalked away. I guess he told me.

But who was paying him to do this job? We were. I was so dumbfounded that, to this day, I still don't know what I should have said, but I wish I'd said something. My guess is he was so tired of catering to so many groups of people who probably slept through a good chunk of his presentations that he decided to tell it like it was. My takeaway was that I should hide closer to the back of the bus and not ask any questions.

We had a lot of fun, and by the end of the trip, everyone was thanking Frank for a great time. Not I. I was still planning how to get even for his quip about falling asleep. Some day I will think of an appropriate response.

Be careful what you wish for... you just might get it

I was invited to an event where I neither wanted to hang out my teeth (fake a smile) nor to make small talk at a painfully long evening surrounded by people I would not normally choose to spend time with.

So, I had slightly fibbed. I offered an apology with a reasonable excuse that my back had been flaring up due to the huge amount of holiday cooking and entertaining. What I did not expect was to end up with an even bigger reason not to attend. While blithely ducking into a grocery, I caught the front of my sneaker on the curb and suddenly realized I was headed face-first toward the fast-approaching pavement. Oh boy!

That was all I had time to process as I landed, splat, having bent back my bad toe, landing on both knees and banging my ribcage in the process. The hands that were supposed to break my fall did only enough to get bruised themselves. And then, as I was lying there with the breath knocked out of me, I realized I was getting to the age my mother was when she started falling down. Oh no! And then: at least my pants aren't ripped! Funny that these were my thoughts before "when will I be able to breathe again" as I lay there so ungracefully by the line-up of grocery carts.

Then came the pain. A lovely woman rushed over and asked, "Would you like some help?" She started to pull on my arm to help me up. "I'd love you to get me a blanket and cover me up right here," I would have said if I could have gotten the words out. Instead, I struggled to hold up a finger to indicate "maybe in a minute."

When I could finally speak, I said, "Thank you, but I just need to gather my wits, which I seem to have scattered all over the place." She offered me my purse and said I should zip it up (thanks Mom), as if theft was of the utmost importance. I noticed my sunglasses had gone flying, but no one could get past the blob on the pavement to step on them. Then, of course, my mind went to, "How many witnesses saw my wonderful display of complete ineptitude at navigating a simple curb?" Embarrassment always rears its head at times like this, even though it is ridiculous to worry about how you look. I could tell I looked like an idiot.

But then I had to get up and get moving, and that is when the damage sank in. I bravely continued on into the grocery store and got what I needed as if the fall hadn't happened, hobbling along as I assessed what hurt most. Apart from my pride, there were the ribs, the hands, the knees—even my teeth seemed off kilter, jarred from the fall, not to mention the toe that had been the cause of it all. Why hadn't it watched where it was going?

Typical of after a trauma, I was sore the first day and miserable by the fourth, contemplating an x-ray. I was told that healing would take two weeks if the ribs were bruised, four if they were cracked and six weeks if they were broken. But there was nothing anyone could do about them anyway, so I would just have to wait and see.

I'd never really appreciated my good health, when I had only one or two ailments to kvetch about. A fall gives one a lot more sense of one's fallibility (pun intended). It also guaranteed my excuse for that evening affair I hadn't wanted to attend. In the end, the fates made sure that if I was going to beg off, I would have an honest reason.

Of course, the real question was, "What if I just didn't want to go?" Full stop. I wonder when I will be old enough to just say it with no guilt whatsoever.

How do you resist the urge to fix?

It's hard to know the right thing to say when someone is struggling with a crisis or a tragedy, a personal loss or disappointment. If a friend is passed over for a promotion they were sure they deserved, or just lost a job they loved, or got dumped by a girlfriend or boyfriend, what do you say? "That's so hard"? Perhaps. "I'm so sorry"? How about, "That just doesn't seem fair."

I once heard someone describe empathy as that ability to climb down into the pit of despair with a friend and just sit quietly with them so they know they are not alone. How hard is that? Empathy is so hard, especially for someone like me who wants to fix the world. I have learned that good suggestions are not what people need when they are feeling blue. They just need to wallow for a bit, until somewhere within themselves they find the answers. But in the meantime, finding the right words of comfort can be a challenge. Sometimes the challenge is just to listen and say, "I hear you," or, as today's generation says, "I feel you."

For people like me who want to fix what's wrong, it can be a very humbling exercise to be told someone does not need your help. Basically, they are saying, "Just shut up and listen." I'm still trying to learn that skill. I wish there were courses on this. You want so badly to help and you wish you knew how. And then there is that wise man who is said to know that the best thing to say is absolutely nothing.

Hmm. That might make a very good tattoo or, next best thing, I could just keep it front and centre in my brain.

So many times, I've wished I'd done just that. They say that when the student is ready, the teacher will appear. I'm still hoping someone will have the fortitude and patience to show me the way. There are so many times I can think back on when I wished I'd just listened. Maybe one has to be much older than I am now to finally get it.

A wise friend said to me, just stick to how you feel for them. "I'm so sorry you are going through this." Express your feelings and then be quiet rather than slipping into judging others. When they are ready, they will come to their own conclusions without you saving their world.

I spend a lot of time walking our wonderful dog, who never says anything but has brought so much joy to our world. She has the hang of how to say nothing. Often, she will just sit beside us and put her head on our lap as a signal to pet her. Now, petting people when they are down will not work. However, one of my dog-walking buddies slipped on black ice when we were out braving the subzero temperatures one morning. My first instinct was to reach down and help her up. But, since I am not a novice when it comes to falling (something I inherited from my late mother, so I blame her), I knew that the best thing to do was sit down beside her. Hauling her up when her world was suddenly turned upside down, literally, was not the answer. So I sat with her while she caught her breath and took stock of anything damaged, and when she was ready, we got up together. Perhaps finding the right thing to say is much like that. Just being there so someone knows they are not alone might be the right thing after all. Nothing said. Just company in a bad moment.

What does one say at a shiva or funeral?

One of the toughest situations is knowing what to say at a shiva (seven days of mourning in the Jewish faith) or a funeral. Not that I hang out at them on a regular basis, but there comes a time for each of us when we are more frequent visitors.

When I was a child, my parents insisted I must go to pay my respects, whatever that meant. I had no idea what to say and would immediately start to whine, "But I don't want to go. I don't even know what to say." My parents, of course, provided platitudes—easy for them, my parents were a hundred years old. An eleven or twelve year old saying they are sorry for your loss just doesn't ring sincere, not even to a child's ear, never mind an adult who is grieving. In what world could I, with all my twelve years of experience, have anything to say that would make someone six or seven times my age feel even a tiny bit better? Most often I said nothing.

Unfortunately, once we've grown up, we can no longer hide behind our youth and inexperience. The time has definitely come to say something. But what? "I'm sure you will miss them," "At least they are no longer in pain," "Well, they are now over the rainbow bridge playing with their friends"? That last one is probably only for the loss of a beloved pet. I can't say a person is romping in greener pastures.

Truth be told, we were taught to not address a mourner at a shiva, nor to take coffee or food unless you provided the shiva meal. Practices in the Jewish faith are more relaxed today, though many of our traditions still have rules and guidelines. It all depends how observant you are. My understanding of the original custom was that you spoke when spoken to by the immediate family that is mourning. If you were accompanying someone like a spouse who knew the family, you introduced yourself and expressed your sorrow to mourners you had not met and got outta there.

A shiva or funeral is a tough time, no matter what, and it's not a social occasion. The thing that makes me absolutely crazy is when visitors use a shiva as a chance to catch up with other visitors, who may be friends they have not seen for a long time. At some shivas I hear conversations about football games and who's watching what on Netflix. I don't make the rules, but it sure seems like a time to speak your condolences and vanish unless you are a very close friend and the mourner wants your company. Perhaps it's a good time to take someone's hand and look sad, the fewer words spoken the better.

At one shiva there was actually a sign on the door that said, "Please respect our desire to have a traditional shiva."

That was what they wished to say, and they said it.

When you miss your chance to say goodbye

There my husband's father lay in bed, day after day, getting slowly weaker by the hour. A sneaking suspicion arose in my heart that this might be "it." The year had been terrible. First, my mother-in-law took sick and was in the hospital for four months. Then my husband's parents moved together to a retirement home with more care so she could have respite care. In the spring, Pops' heart began to run out of steam, which it can do at the age of ninety-eight. All he wanted was to get out of hospital and be home with his wife for his birthday.

After the doctors told us to gather the family, my father-in-law fooled everyone by making a remarkable recovery. He got his wish. We celebrated his birthday with the entire family crowded into their living room. Though Pops had gained back some strength, he was still much weakened. The rubber ball never bounces as high as that first bounce, but enough that my husband and I were rebooking the trip overseas that we had canceled in May.

By late August, all seemed okay—until it wasn't. My father-in-law said he was not feeling well. The palliative care team seemed unconcerned, yet something was definitely wrong. After a hurried ambulance ride to the hospital, an emergency doctor confirmed that his heart was failing. We all had great faith he would rally one more time, as he always seemed to regain enough strength and sheer will to come home from the hospital. But what if he didn't?

Each day we visited. Each day we hoped and prayed, but it became obvious to me that even the excellent bedside care from personal support workers, combined with his enormous determination, wasn't going to be enough.

As he lay there amid the tangle of blankets and sheets, tubes and beeping machinery, I could see he was getting weaker. He even told the care worker he was "going." When was the right time to say goodbye? If I told him I loved him and would miss him and talked about all the happy times we had shared, would that make him give up?

Years before, I had learned so much about this remarkable man sitting with him in the early morning hours at the hospital, and again at rehab, when he had broken his shoulder falling down the stairs. He had so many interesting stories to tell. He stood first in his graduating pharmacy class at the University of Toronto. He won the gold medal. He couldn't receive his degree until later in May, after he turned twenty-one. He had owned and worked at many local pharmacies and knew every pharmacist in the city as a long-time member of his fraternity. I treasured that time of getting to know him. I loved his stories. I loved his humility. No one knew what the gold medal was on the edge of his degree, leaning against the wall in the dusty basement. He was so modest.

The care worker kept up a steady chatter and tried to get him to move his limbs to "limber up." She played show tunes on her cell phone and pretended to dance with him. Pops loved the theatre, music, dance and the opera. I thought about exactly when I would say what I wanted to say. I didn't want him to think I was hurrying him on his journey, but all the signs were there. Even the medical staff seemed to stop trying. If you are lucky enough to have a parent who is ninety-eight years old, there's a good chance you are in your seventies. By this age, most of us have lost a parent or two and a good many friends too. At his age he had attended so many funerals of his friends and even younger family members.

Part of me was definitely in denial. If I said nothing then maybe he would make it. I couldn't seem to get the words out, as much as I wanted to say them.

I regret that now. Having known him for only twenty-five years, my loss was nothing compared to that of my husband, who was fortunate enough to still have both his parents when he was in his seventies. They say there is no good time to lose a parent. I know. I lost one when I was in my twenties and the other when I was in my fifties. It's true that each is painful, no matter how long or short the time you have had with them.

All those things I wish I'd said. Thank you for the opportunity to get to know you. Thank you for sharing your stories with me and listening to mine. I loved every one of your adventures. I loved you, even if it was for a relatively short time. You were a good man and you and your beloved wife raised a great son; I am ever so grateful for that and for the wonderful values and traditions you instilled.

Better late than never, they say. Wherever my father-in-law is now, I am sure he understands how I felt.

The basement of so many memories

Engaging others in your much desired project of cleaning out the basement is one of those things. After you've invited them to help—more like pleaded, begged, cajoled, bribed and guilted—you wish you'd just done it yourself. No matter how much you insist, persist and threaten, there is always another agenda aside from yours. As Stephen Covey said in his book *Seven Habits of Highly Effective People,* "If you don't have your own agenda you will become part of someone else's." In my book, it's right up there with, "Failing to plan is planning to fail." My husband often mimics me when I spout the latter, which he has heard so often.

So it was with great hopes that I announced my desire to finally get rid of the green carpeting in the basement and put down some kind of wood flooring, real or faux, to bring our house into the twenty-first century.

It started a year and a half ago with the simple desire to turn one room into a playroom for the grandchildren so they would have a space to disappear to. Although, if you think about it, the whole point of having them over is to spend time with them, especially when that time is so short and fleeting. Nevertheless, a designated play area seemed like a good idea, somewhere they could go wild with impunity.

Who knew that eighteen months after my original request, I would be reading the riot act to recalcitrant family members who were clearly not on board with my plans. Instead of taking their stuff out of said basement and finding a new home for it (not in ours, please), I was still ranting and raving about how everyone had been given ample notice. Now it was past time for it all to go ... to Goodwill, Value Village, their own homes, to the garbage or the recycling depot. I didn't particularly care, as long as it went. I figured if this stuff hadn't been touched for twenty years, and more was smuggled in when we weren't looking, a clean-out was long past due.

Then came the arguing among family members. "This wasn't mine, it was yours." And so the box sat, unclaimed. To be sure, my husband had added to one son's boxes and another son was smuggling in their kids' outgrown clothing in the event a younger cousin might share their fashion taste. Then there were the toys and accoutrements one gathers for when the grandchildren come over: riding toys, learning-to-walk toys, counting toys, rocking chairs and strollers just in case. Every time I ventured into that room, one or another toy would suddenly speak up or start singing a nursery rhyme, scaring me out of my wits with "Sing along with me" or "Let's play a game!" Yes, let's. It's called murder in the dark.

The problem with this clutter, wherever it piles up (my husband's former household had a dedicated "box room"), is that taking the first step in parting with the past is often an emotional tug of war. You know you won't ever use those six briefcases, but someone important gave them to you, so there is sentimental value. Large, framed pictures of milestone moments, such as bar mitzvahs, are especially tough to discard; not one of our kids wanted theirs, so we now had at least two giant ones of each child, thanks to some long-deceased grandparents. I brought home other treasures when cleaning out relatives' homes, thinking maybe one day the kids will want them. Guess what! They don't, and they won't—but they'll never admit it.

Whether you plan to die in your home or downsize to a condo, the exercise of clearing out is daunting. And who wants to leave this to someone else after you're gone? They won't even ponder whether something is worth keeping. One call to Zip Junk and it will be gone.

Meanwhile, how is it that, when it is time to get rid of unwanted furniture, everyone in the family has a bad back? When family was visiting from out of town and the talk turned to lending a hand to get the stuff to the curb, there were so many bad backs! Discussions of MRIS, CT scans, x-rays and hip replacements are common among my age group, but the thirty-somethings? It's hard to imagine.

This is not a problem I face alone. Some of my friends are going through this exact process. Everyone groans when you bring up the subject of cleaning out the basement. One friend decided to clean everything out of her house before she is too old and decrepit to do it. Her husband, who is not on the same page, has announced that by the time she is seventy there will be nothing left to throw out.

I have decided on a new policy about leaving stuff in our home. I will set up a screening device inside the front door that automatically announces, "Are you bringing that in? Do you plan to take it home when you leave? If not, you are not allowed in." That should just about do it.

Seriously though, in the future I will quietly get rid of all the junk without any discussion. If someone asks where is their beloved Wubby, I will just tell them I have no idea.

When I really should say "Yes!"

My husband offers me help all the time. I say no. Why? Am I a martyr? Do I like making dinner every night? And looking after the garden? And always being the one to buy the gifts for his family?

When company comes, who worries and frets, shopping and cooking for days on end? And that does not include Rosh Hashanah dinner and the Passover Seder, Chanukah standing over a hot frying pan cooking latkes by the dozen. I do the lion's share of the laundry and the groceries.

What am I, a masochist? I guess so.

I also do all of the arranging for plumbers, electricians and other tradespeople. This may be a carryover from the sixteen years I lived on my own, when I created a rolodex of phone numbers, which I've continued to craft over many years. And I do feel quite competent and capable handling all these tasks, which, by the way, I also did when I worked full time.

But from time to time, I come back with my gunny sack and let my husband have it. Why am I doing all the work? Why am I so exhausted? You go to work all day, which you love, leaving everything else in the house on my shoulders.

"And whose fault is that?" I ask myself when I am in my right mind. Why do I do this? What is wrong with me that I take on so much? Why am I the one planning the vacations and the meals? It's not as if he doesn't travel with me or eat three meals a day. And yet ...

Somewhere along the way, I learned that, when there was a need, I should either jump in and lend a hand or just do it all myself. If there is a problem, fix it. A friend shared some advice her grandmother gave her when she got married. She said don't be so quick to jump in and do it all. What's the rush? Let it all sit for a day or two or three and see if anyone else notices that something is needed.

I've been trying that out lately.

A longtime friend of mine has also had it with plugging in. It took her about seventy-five years to realize that if someone else can do it, let them. Her mother is elderly and needs care. Whenever there is no one available, Lorna plugs herself in. She has not had a Saturday night to herself in years. And when her dad was alive it was the same thing. She is very close to burned out, but now she has gotten smart, she tells me. If it is not something only a daughter can handle, she's assigning the work to someone else.

My sister, a retired psychologist who practised in California and whom I just saw for the first time in five years, said that doing everything myself is a system I set up. Now I want to change part of the system. No wonder I get push-back, she said.

I had no idea what she was talking about, but then she is a family therapist, so I should probably trust that she knows a thing or two. The thing about younger sisters is that no matter how mature we get, we hate being told what to do by an older sister. And so, I resist.

It does make sense that I have conditioned everyone around me to count on me to plug in, fill in and jump in. I am now revising that impulse. Today. I am taking a step back and asking, "Whose problem is it?" If it isn't really mine, I am giving up the task of fixing. I am no longer saying, "Here I'll do it." I'm waiting to see if anyone else will. Ah, but it is so tempting because then I get to do it my way.

No. I will not. I am sitting on my hands and keeping shtum (quiet), as another friend says. Let's see how long I can hold out.

Letting go

In a previous book I talked about how our perspective changes as we age. I wrote a chapter asking when it is time for the kids to take over all the celebratory dinners and events, pondering if I should pass the torch. I decided that it was, indeed, time, and I took my own advice. That year, I announced I was not making Rosh Hashanah dinner. If the kids wanted dinner, someone else would have to make it.

I was only half serious. I was actually annoyed at something said offspring had done, and this was my version of a sit-down strike. It didn't hurt that my back had been killing me for weeks, making the thought of another three weeks of cooking seem impossible. It was then that I added up just how many years I had been preparing these meals and reached the conclusion, "Oh for heaven's sake, give it up already. Get a life. Do other things with the time you have now created. Enjoy not standing on your feet for three weeks." Hmm. Now there's a thought.

What I discovered was that it is not so easy to let go of the reigns. I started to worry. What would dinner look like? Should I offer to bring a dish, as I had always wanted them to do when invited to a dinner? Would that be offending them? In other words, how do I let go and trust that, while dinner may not be what I would serve, it would be just fine. After all, it was not the last supper, so to speak. There would be a meal the next day, perhaps even three, and I could decide exactly how those meals would look and taste.

Never mind that none of the kids has a dining room or a place for us all to sit at a table together. So what if it won't be a formal sit down, those are vastly overrated. So what if we are sitting on the floor or the couch arms or on the counter. I have been told over and over that no one comes for the food. They come to be together, and isn't that what is most important of all?

Maybe so. But in my mind, that togetherness has always been enhanced by the quality of the food. Then again, none of these kids is a gourmet eater. Between the one with the allergies to nuts and the other allergic to eggs, cooking for this crew has never been easy. Two are eaters, the others, not so much. So, who exactly am I cooking all this food for every year, anyway? I suspect for my mother, who has been long gone, along with the chance of her approval.

It's hard to let go. It's hard to acknowledge that, once our generation is gone, the next one will have its own ideas of what to serve, how to serve it or whether to even have a Rosh Hashanah dinner. None of this do I have any control over. And so, in spite of the fact that I was not entirely serious when I suggested someone other than I make this year's New Year's dinner, my comment was taken seriously and the wheels were set in motion.

Whatever it turns out to be, I am sure the holiday celebration will be lovely. It's really hard to sit on my hands and do nothing, say nothing and even think nothing. I'm working on it. And perhaps when it is time to do the dishes, my husband and I can quietly slip away—after all, we really should have been in bed ages ago, we old folk. Wink wink.

The kinder may surprise you after all

I gave up the reigns and, hallelujah, one very brave son and daughter-in-law picked them up and ran with them. Rosh Hashanah dinner that year was at their home, and it was unbelievable. If it hadn't been good (and I was afraid it wouldn't be), my plan was to bite my tongue and enjoy it, even if it killed me. "Keep your comments to yourself," my friends had counseled. I thought I would feel useless not doing all the cooking and slaving in the kitchen for days on end. I was sure it would not feel like home, or *haymishe*, if it wasn't in our dining room. Boy, was I wrong.

The next generation not only took on Operation First Night Rosh Hashanah, they hit it out of the ballpark. I was totally blown away. First there was salami on the grill. Okay, so they didn't take off the plastic on the outside. My husband ate it anyway. Mini hot dogs in pastry. Veggies and dips. Fries for the little ones. For the big ones, chicken soup and matzo balls, then meatballs and honey garlic wings, sauteed peppers and pulled lamb with pitas. Two different kinds of salads, potatoes and broccoli.

Our host and hostess were so busy serving, clearing, cooking, plating and cleaning, and in a very small kitchen, that they didn't sit down for one moment. They were juggling all the different dishes that needed to be heated up in an oven that could not accommodate them all at once. Dan had made his bubbie's honey cake recipe, and she agreed he nailed it. He had food for those who couldn't eat eggs, nut-free for those who were allergic. White wine, red wine, grape juice for kiddush and challah for the blessing over the bread. Pomegranate and apple, with different kinds of honey for dipping, to ensure a sweet New Year. The dinner really was spectacular.

We were all beaming. How heartwarming to have four generations together, from age two to ninety-five. The table, a section of which was borrowed from the condo party room downstairs, was beautiful, laid with their very best china and flatware, beautifully lit, with centrepieces and all. I'm sure they had enough food for fifty, but we were only twelve. Lots to take home in care packages. How odd, the offspring giving the aging parents care packages to take home. Now there's a switch.

I learned a lot that night, and so did the kids. Bite your tongue and say nothing, was my lesson, while they learned how much work goes into a dinner like this; now they know why I was not at our table for very long over the years. I understand they worked on this for a good few weeks, trying out recipes, testing, tasting, and it showed. Four hours into the dinner, they were exhausted.

I was so proud of them, and told them so. I left reassured that, after our generation is gone, the tradition will live on. How gratifying to learn that they were paying attention all along. I may not be done hosting forever, but it was a relief after forty years of making holiday dinners that I could have this one off and be a guest. It did not feel like I had missed anything at all, except the sore back and muscles from standing on my feet for weeks, preparing. At one point I tried to help in the kitchen and was promptly, but nicely, told to get out. After all, my daughter-in-law was quick to point out, look how hard I had worked on the many dinners I prepared and served to them. That was the nicest of compliments, and I will cherish it forever.

Instead of worrying and feeling bad that I was not hosting this year, I wish I'd said earlier that I had confidence in their ability to carry the evening off with panache and that I was so looking forward to it—so much so that I am hoping for a repeat performance next year. I could get very used to this.

The Bundt cake

As the mom in *My Big Fat Greek Wedding* famously asked, "What is this Bundt?" In my case it had been a family tradition passed down to me by my mom, who was an excellent cook and baker. I even have her original Bundt pan. She would make a marble cake in this pan that surpassed all others, in my opinion, and I don't remember this ever being one of her kitchen flops. (She did have a few. See my first book, *It All Ends Up in a Parfait Glass*.)

Imagine my surprise when I finally tried my hand at this cake and, even after six attempts (not all at the same time), could never get it out of the pan. I tried cooking spray, oil and greasing it with Crisco (if anyone even remembers that stuff; it came in a cardboard rectangle wrapped in waxed paper and was used in all kinds of pies and cakes). No matter what I greased the pan with, the cake always stuck to it and no amount of coercion would coax it out in one clean piece. I tried putting the baked cake in a container of hot water. I tried a spatula. I even resorted to hiding the broken bits with icing. Sorry, Mom, I know it never had icing in your day, but needs must, as the

British say. I refused to toss the cake out no matter how bad it looked.

Another ingredient the recipe called for was Coffee Rich. I asked at the local grocery store and was sent first to the coffee aisle and then to the egg department. No one seemed to know of this product. After asking five or six store clerks, I asked to speak with the manager. An older gentleman came over and said he knew exactly what I wanted. Hurray. As he walked me over to the freezer, he said, "You know, this product is from long ago." And I'm thinking, "I guess I am too."

These youngsters don't really know about products from way back when. I explained that my recipe was from way back when too, feeling a distinct camaraderie with my new buddy, the store manager. He was younger than I by at least a decade, but I was not going to say anything about that. I also didn't say what I was thinking: I wonder if these young folk even bake or cook anymore?

I have decided that whatever magic touch my mom had with the Bundt cake, I did not inherit it along with the recipe, so I have determined the pan will have to go and I will use another type of Bundt pan. And yet, I hesitate. Tradition and nostalgia make me reluctant to relinquish this bit of my past. Should I give it one more try? My hairdresser says to fit parchment paper inside the pan.

What I wish I'd done is asked more questions of my mom when she was in the kitchen so many years ago. Some guidance from above would be really helpful. Next time the curio cabinet door opens, perhaps I can ask?

P.S. Not to be beaten by a ridiculous baking pan, I tried the recipe again in my own Bundt pan, and guess what? That cake came out beautifully. Sorry, Mom, your pan is going to Goodwill. Right after we taste this newly shaped version at this year's Rosh Hashanah dinner.

Sniffing out the right nose

With all the animation today that's elevated to an art form, it's nice to know that some of the old favourites still resonate with a new generation. Our almost-three-year-old granddaughter has discovered Snoopy. So in love is she with these characters that she is having a Snoopy birthday party.

I remembered that, in return for me babysitting some young cousins in my teens, their mom and dad brought me a Snoopy dog from FAO Schwartz, which in those days was the gold standard for toys and stuffed animals, as it continued to be for many years. Maybe still is. My cousins had asked me what size sweater I wore before they left for New York City. To avoid such a gift, I told them I had lots of sweaters. Maybe that was rude, but when they returned from their trip, they handed me an authentic FAO Shwartz Snoopy. Now, *that* was a great thank-you gift.

My little cousins were five and seven at the time, a girl and a boy. The girl delighted in taking off her shoes and socks and inviting her feet onto the dinner table where she would exclaim, "Toro, wild footsies!" I loved it. The boy, who decided I was his first big crush, would not let go of me when it was time to tuck him in. There were stories, and more stories, and finally hugs and kisses, but he would wrap his arms around me as if he was never going to let go. Heady stuff for a fifteen-year-old with no younger siblings.

We spent a good two weeks frolicking at the cottage in the water, learning to swim (they, not I), going to movies and playing games. I loved bonding with those two. Receiving a gorgeous Snoopy was the icing on the cake that summer.

Snoopy had pride of place on my childhood bed with all my other beloved animals. And when I finally married, had a home, and storage space, Snoopy came with me from one house to the next. I knew my Snoopy was still pretty white and fluffy, down in our furnace room, neatly packed away for a rainy day or whenever I needed to take a trip down memory lane.

Now, finally, after seven decades, I pulled him out of storage. He looked pretty good, though he was dusty and smelled like he had been in a box for a long time. If I was going to introduce him to my granddaughter, I thought it would be a good idea to give him a swimming lesson, so off he went into the washing machine. Although I did not risk putting him in the dryer, somehow his nose came off and disappeared.

Sparkling white and clean (though still without a nose), Snoopy was now ready to meet my very eager little one. She had become quite attuned to body parts and all their functions. In her serious, almost-three-year-old vocabulary, she said to me, "Bubbie, can you go to the Snoopy dog nose store and get a new nose for Snoopy?" How darling! And how intent she was in getting Snoopy his nose. I loved it. I promised I would, and then had to scour the city's fabric and craft stores.

I didn't find just one nose. They were sold in packs of fifty. Black furry balls the perfect size for a nose. I was thrilled that I could grant her wish. After sewing on the nose, I called her mom.

"Is Rachel there?"

"Sorry, she is having her nap."

"Okay," I countered. "When she gets up can you tell her that Bubbie went to the Snoopy dog nose store and got Snoopy a new nose?" Such a little request from such a wonderful little girl warmed my heart. It made me feel so connected to my grandchild to know I could grant this wish for her. I think it was the first time she had ever asked me for anything. Pretty special.

Snoopy is still mine, you see. Rachel can play with him only when she is here at our house. But I think we have found her another Snoopy dog, just the right size for her little arms. I can't wait until her birthday to see her delight when she receives her very own Snoopy dog.

As for the forty-nine remaining black fluff balls, I'm told our grandcat would be delighted to chase a few around. That leaves forty-six. Anyone have a stuffed animal that needs a nose replaced? Free to a good home.

Starting off on the wrong foot

"Who gets a foot massage?"

That's what my husband asked when his friends Matt and Lorna invited us to kick off our Saturday evening by doing just that.

"You'll love it," they insisted. "It's so relaxing." Matt assured us that the experience was so wonderful he often fell asleep. We agreed to give it a go.

We arrived at the Massage Clinic as it was called and were amazed at the foot traffic. People were lining up to go inside. "What's the big attraction?" I wondered. I'd seen firsthand (or first foot) the places in Thailand that advertised the virtues of fish nibbling at your toes. No thank you, that I could live without. But our friends assured us that this place was a bonafide (though not registered) establishment where we would be well looked after.

In the foyer, we were greeted with glasses of tea and ice-cold water to quench our thirst until our room was available. So far so good. At the appointed hour, three masseurs and one masseuse greeted us and invited us into a darkened room where soft, subtle music was playing. There was a large television on the wall, but we all agreed we would do without this particular distraction.

The process started with a foot soak in special oak buckets. Matt, who said he enjoyed this so much, had such large feet they had to find a special bucket to accommodate them. After our feet had been soaking for a while, our masseurs dried our legs and feet with towels and applied massage cream.

This was my husband's first massage—ever—so he had no idea what to expect. He's funny about his feet, though. Hates to go barefoot, never wears sandals, prefers lace-ups to slip-ons. "Never mind," as my mother would say. "He has other good qualities." That's why I was surprised he would let a stranger near his feet, never mind massage them.

Each masseur had their own style, four of them working on eight feet. I'm not sure if they were registered or had any training. Once my husband's masseur got started, it looked like he was trying to twist his foot right off his body. My husband had a pained expression on his face, as if to say, "When will this be over?" His masseur kept looking at the ceiling, so Jay looked up too to see what was so interesting. As the masseur began twisting Jay's toes one by one, Jay was clearly distressed, as if his masseur might be trying to break them off his feet altogether.

He was not having a good time. I, on the other hand, promptly told my masseuse that she was using far too much pressure and asked her to ease off a bit, so I did not leave looking like bruised fruit. Her enthusiasm was all well and good, but I detest deep tissue massage of any kind. I did not want to discover new aches and pains along with the ones I already had. As none of the staff spoke English, it took a few minutes and some pantomiming to get my point across. My masseuse got the message, and I got a strange but somewhat relaxing massage.

Sadly, my husband was far too polite to say anything. Bet he wished he had, as he did not enjoy his first massage at all. In fact, to this day when he wants to suggest an evening out, he jokingly asks, "How about a foot massage?"

Thanks, but let's not get off on the wrong foot. Dinner out will be just fine with me.

Speaking of friends we meet through our dogs

When I was raising a daughter, I often became friends with the parents of her friends. Now that I am a dog owner, I make friends with other dog owners. It's natural. We have a common interest, our fur babies. We count on these friends for walks and doggie advice on training and health issues: How do I find a good vet? Where is the best groomer? Is doggie insurance a good bet or a costly gamble?

And then we branch out into books and movies, the theatre, travels. We have met a lot of famous people through our pets, but on the street they are just ordinary dog-loving citizens. Need a dentist? We have a good one. Need a good doctor who's taking new patients? Pure gold. Lots of good recommendations.

Need your dog walked while you are laid up with an illness? These friends have got you covered. My neighbour was fantastic years ago when I tore my ACL (ligament at the top of the knee). For six weeks he faithfully took my dog out for a walk, no matter the weather. Other friends brought along their dog and took mine to the dog park for a run. Every Saturday. I can't express how grateful I am that they were there for me. Dog people are the best.

We look out for each other. Such was the case when Jim and I met, he with his husky, me with my first wheaten terrier. The dogs were okay with each other, but Jim and I bonded over common interests. He was a fascinating guy, well read, well traveled, sharp, informed and kind. We would meet on a street corner and proceed on our walk together. No heavy discussions, just companionship on a freezing cold day when only idiots, fools and dog owners were out. We met at the dog park, where most of the women were on one side and most of the men on the other. I was friends with both camps.

One spring day, many months after I had met Jim, I saw a woman named Kay leaving the park with Jim's dog.

"Where are you going with Jim's dog?" I asked. The incredulous answer came back right away, "This is my dog."

"No, it's not. It Jim's!" I said, knowing perfectly well that it was.

"Yes," she replied, "and Jim is my husband!"

Who knew? Not I. It never dawned on me that the two were married.

So you never know who you will meet while walking your dog. Dogs open up a whole new world of relationships. I know that the two years between pets, when our first had gone over the rainbow bridge and the second was not yet born, I felt completely cut off from my neighbourhood. I didn't know who was moving in or out, who was selling, who became a grandparent and who the new doggies in the 'hood were.

When we got our new puppy, she was such a loving and good-natured citizen (a relief from the criminal we had harboured for fifteen years) that we immediately introduced her to all kinds of new doggie friends. For some reason, remembering doggie names is easy, but we can't always remember names of their owners. But names or not, we do have a special bond, cherished membership in a unique club. Nothing needs to be said. We all understand each other perfectly.

Meet my dog... and who are you, again?

Out walking one bright, sunny day in May, I came across a woman with her golden retriever, Percy. We bump into each other all the time and have become good friends. We always talk about our dogs, but we also talk books, current events, weekend plans and, of course, the weather (no conversation in Canada gets going without the weather)—everything from the philosophical to the mundane.

On this particular day I was with another friend, and as is customary, the time came to introduce them. I was stuck. Percy, the golden, I could introduce to Micky, the Westie mix. But I was at a loss to introduce Percy's mom to my friend, as I did not know her name. Thankfully, they exchanged names themselves, and I gave mine too.

What struck me is that a community of dogs is really all about the dogs, not the owners. The humans are important, but I guess the dogs are more so. Not only do I remember dog names, I even know which dog can have chicken treats and who will only eat beef. I know the ones that can't be fed treats at all due to allergies. I know who's on a special diet and who got bitten by a raccoon recently.

I'm very concerned about my dog's friendships. Is this one friendly? Is that one going to suddenly turn and snarl? Some dogs you just know need a wide berth. Others' tails are wagging the minute they see you coming. Yet others hit the deck as if they are saying, "You can't see me if I get really flat to the ground." Most dog owners who have spent time training their four-legged citizens will know this is a shy dog without a lot of confidence; they are hiding in the only way they know how, and they are not going to cause trouble.

Then there are the dog owners who give *you* a wide berth because either their dog is very badly behaved, given to lunging and biting, or your dog is, and they are doing their best to avoid you. You'll have to watch carefully for another telltale sign that an approaching dog is not friendly: the owner will begin to wind their end of the leash around their fist until the dog has no latitude to do any of his bad-behaviour routines. I look for that signal and cross the road.

I've had both types of dogs, one badly trained (my fault), and one a little angel, partly because I had her bred to specification and partly because I invested a lot of time in proper dog training and handling. Both were the same breed from the same kennel. One was on the city's most wanted list several times.

Once, a neighbour posted a picture of my sweet, loving boy, asking if anyone had seen him, like he was a common criminal. Seems she was concerned about her twenty-nine-year-old son who, when jogging, had been nipped by my little criminal as he ran too close to him. He should have known better. The jogger, not my precious dog, who was only reacting out of fear. You can't run right up behind a dog, step on its hind foot and not expect a reaction. I should have said that. And furthermore, what twenty-nine-year-old needs his mom to go after said criminal on his behalf?

Seems the difference between a well-behaved dog and a badly behaved one is all in the training. And it's not the dog that's being trained. It's the human. There's a reason trainers won't take your dog, perhaps wild and crazy as a new pup, and give you back a perfectly charming companion. It's because if the owner is not involved, the dog will only be good for the trainer they have learned to obey. And, after all, a dog is a blank slate and takes behaviour cues from us humans. How we train the humans to behave is a totally different issue. Maybe instead of minding other people's business, that mom could have taught her runner son how to behave around dogs.

My husband is like a very well-trained dog. He never puts a foot wrong. Goes into a room full of people carefully, cautiously, and assesses the situation before he opens his mouth. He does not need to be the centre of attention. He is quite happy to be one of the gang. When he contributes, he will be funny and charming, but he has no need to dominate the situation. It's quite a relief, actually, from all those people who demand you look at them, talk about their lives and make them the centre of the action. They can be exhausting. Not my husband. He is naturally quiet, well behaved and a good listener.

Our dog adores him. All weekend long, she stays close to her worship-worthy god. She will curl up next to him on the couch or the bed. Wherever he is, she is a snuggle distance away. They both love it that way.

Then comes Monday when he goes back to work. Adoring puppy becomes miserable and withdrawn, completely ignoring the fact that I feed her, I walk her and I am the one shoving medicine down her throat and taking her to the vet when she needs to go. Yet I become, as they say, chopped liver.

That's gratitude for you.

When my husband reaches for the keys to his car, which he worships, doggie is already heading for the door, prancing and spinning and barking. When they leave with the top down, she is hanging off the back of the rear seat as if to say, "Here we go! Wind in my fur, Daddy at the helm, life is perfect."

Oh, to be a dog and enjoy the simple pleasures of life. They don't really care what your name is like we humans do, but they know a good heart almost instantly. As a dear friend once said, "A heart knows a heart." They think we are perfect just as we are. Wish more people would try to live up to that.

Oh, to be young and driving the seniors home

I am astounded today at the bravado and confidence of youth. I shouldn't be surprised, though, as I was that way myself. How does the joke go? Get a teenager to do it while they still know everything. What happens between being confident teenagers who know everything and fifty years later, when we know all that can go wrong? Experience. And it can be sobering.

Nevertheless, at barely nineteen years of age, while waiting to go back to university, I was working for the nation's capital Social Planning Council on Senior Citizens' Week. My job was to promote the events widely, which meant doing a lot of research to get names of organizations and their addresses. I don't know what the council did with all the information, but they seemed to like me enough that after the big event, they lent me out to cover the desk at Big Brothers of Canada. I think I answered the phone while a staff member went on holidays for two weeks. I didn't need to share space with anyone and I had a new park where I could spend time at lunch.

The details of that four-month stint escape me. But what I do remember is that one afternoon in early June, the Senior Citizens' Council actually met, and the office was inundated with the blue-haired set, as I called them to myself. They were all lovely and capable and pretty sharp, but also pretty old to my youthful eye.

After the meeting, around 4 p.m. on a Friday afternoon, my boss casually asked if I could drive four of the women home to the other side of town. He tossed me the keys to his car and quipped nonchalantly, "You can drive standard, can't you?"

"Of course," I smiled, lying through my teeth. Ha! My experience driving a standard car was maybe one or two sessions with a friend who owned a pale blue Pinto. It had been a while ago, but I was sure that driving around an empty parking lot after the mall was closed equipped me to get these women safely home.

Once everyone was belted in, three in the back seat, one in the front with me, I put the key in the ignition, forgetting about the clutch and the need to ever so carefully let it out while I slipped the car into gear. Here I was, in a strange car, in a strange part of the city, with no clue how to drive this car. Yet, my feeling was "I can do this." Jerking and jumping along, I finally got the car in the right gear and headed for the on ramp of the highway. Once on it, I remembered how to shift gears and, in spite of protestations from the back seat, I knew we were good to go.

By the time I hit the off ramp, my passengers were begging to be let out. "I'll just take the bus. It's no problem," they protested.

"No, no, no. I promised to take you home and I will. Now who lives where?" With a few directions from the peanut gallery, I managed to get everyone home. "What was the big deal?" I thought.

Sailing back to the office to return my boss's car, I felt pretty good about my mission. The next day, while I did not expect praise, I also did not expect my boss to say he had received no fewer than four phone calls, all of which specified that I was never to drive them home again. Ever!

Now that I am a lot older and have aches and pains just getting out of my bed or a chair, I realize what an ordeal it must have been for those seniors with fragile, brittle bones, not to mention how hard a novice standard driver is on anyone's nerves.

What was it that Ford said? "If you think you can or you think you can't, you're right"? I probably should have fessed up that I was inexperienced with a stick shift, but what teenager recognizes their own limitations when they want to seem capable and competent? Honestly, I had no idea that I might have been putting those poor seniors at risk in a way I would never do today.

Apart from the guilt that came some fifty years late, I try to focus on the lighter side and practically howl every time I remember that Friday afternoon rush hour when I drove those seniors home, grinding gears, and possibly bones. To be sure, I won't be getting in the car with any teenagers in the too-near future. However, when my grandkids start to drive . . .

Tongs very much

There's a popular bagel shop not too far from where I live. It's been around for years and has a wide assortment of the soft, doughy kind of bagel known as Toronto-style. There's another version from Montreal, and the debate about which city's bagels are better has been going on for decades. I think it depends where that particular Jewish population originally hailed from. The point is that this particular store, once part of a chain, decided to break away and reinvent itself. Just the name. Not the bagels. We were in the habit of buying our challah for Friday night shabbat dinner there, along with an assortment of desserts. I say "were" because it is a rare occasion for me to go in and buy anything now. I am staging a one-woman protest.

Chances are pretty good that if you treat me poorly as a customer I will vote with my feet and not come back. Such were the circumstances after I asked the owner why our challah tasted like bleach. My Friday night guests and I agreed. They must have washed down the bread boards and sat the loaves on them when they came out of the oven. What other rational reason could there be? So I took it upon myself to let the owner know.

What would have been a good response to my query about why the challah tasted like bleach? You would think, "Oh I am so sorry. Let me refund your money. Please take anything you like in the store to compensate you for your inconvenience, your embarrassment and for being so loyal for many, many years."

Who am I kidding? He looked at me and pronounced, "You don't like it? Shop somewhere else!" And so I do. Some of the time. Maybe I am a hypocrite, but the bagels are good, and over the years I have forgiven him, especially since he passed away and his family now runs the store.

At the time, I thought, "Who taught this guy customer service? What happened to "the customer is always right, even when they are wrong"? How about knowing what side your bread is buttered on, or for that matter your bagel? Or "You attract more bees with honey than you do with vinegar?" Clearly, he had not grown up in my household. Some lessons you never forget.

Many years later, a friend who was in from out of town wanted a particular kind of bagel that could only be found at this store. I was going in with her anyway, so I picked up a few bagels with one of the many pairs of tongs hanging on the shelf. By the time I went to pay I had moved the tongs onto my wrist like a shopping bag so I would not drop any of the items I was buying.

Off we went with our purchases, and when we got to my car, I realized I still had the tongs on my arm. No one had said a word. Now the quandary. Do I go back and return them, looking extremely klepto-foolish? Or do I get in the car and drive away?

I figured the latter was the solution. If the owner didn't want to refund my challah purchase from twenty years ago, fine. I'd show him. I'd keep his tongs. Fair is fair and they were probably the same price. If you cross me, you can bet I will get even. If it takes twenty years. What is it the French say? Revenge is a dish best served cold. And bagels taste so much better when you have tongs for serving them.

The self-phone generation

I've been doing some research lately. It's not based on any statistical evidence other than to say these are my observations, and mine alone, although others may have been thinking along the same lines. Years ago, when I was working full time in public relations, I mentioned to a co-worker that I observed real harm being done by the onset of cell phones. As a professional communicator, I commented that I thought the fibre of society was about to unravel. For all the emphasis we place on communication, along comes technology with a means to communicate more and better. But that did not happen. All of the ills I predicted are now coming to real life.

Walking my dog through the park this morning, I spied a youngster, maybe two years old, spinning on a circular apparatus. Every time he went around the circle he would look for his mom's adoring attention, just as we used to swing on the swings and look back to see if the most important person in the world was watching. "Look at me," we would say if we were already talking. The look on this child's face said exactly that.

The warm reflection of a mom's love would come back, either unspoken or spoken, "Look what you can do. Aren't you terrific!"

You don't need a psychology degree to figure out that when the parent is watching and shows an interest, pride or love in the child's success at a small achievement, there is great benefit to that child.

This child came around again and again, looking up at the parent—who was busy looking not at her son but at her cell phone. I felt sad for the child. I didn't know him, but I could understand the disappointment he must have felt as no one watched his mastery of this particular apparatus. I wanted to yell out, "I see you. My doggie sees you. Good on you for figuring that out." Not my job. Not my business. But how sad that mom was not paying attention.

At lunch earlier today in a small local restaurant, I marveled at a young woman, in her twenties I'm guessing, who sat with her mother and perhaps an older sister or aunt. While the other two were engaged in a deep discussion, the twenty-something was busy looking at herself in her cell phone, adjusting her hair, posing and taking pictures of herself.

What is it about cell phones? If all the adults are using them, kids aspire to have them too. And so this cell phone addiction proliferates.

I am baffle-gabbed at this use of what I call self-phones because it is really all about the selfie. What happened to taking pictures of the fabulous world out there? Now everyone puts themselves in the frame instead of just taking in the natural beauty of the attraction. Now it is only valid if you are in the picture too and you send it off to be shared in the public domain. There is a whole industry of "influencers" out there, some with hundreds of thousands of followers. I have no idea how they became such. Advertisers are paying to be on their sites. Yes, the world is changing.

For all our talk about the value of good communication, the cell phone has given us exactly the opposite. It has isolated us more and broken down our ability to have a connection with people in person. Psychologists have realized this. They know that FOMO (fear of missing out) is a real thing. How ironic that the very thing we humans are using to connect is causing more isolation than ever before and resulting in the loss of our ability to actually connect with others in person. No question, a cell phone is a lifesaver in the event of a crisis or accident. But day to day, it is an addiction.

The schools have finally caught on to the damage of cell phones in the classroom. Disruptors all. Banning cell phones in the classroom is a hot new debate, a political football for sure.

How often do you see young people, and older ones too, sitting at a table of four, each on their phone? Go to a sporting event and they are watching the same event up close on their phones or posting their photo of being at the game. How can we regain focus and attention when we are so scattered?

With Artificial Intelligence and ChatGPT so available, where will reality fit? ChatGPT can do your thinking for you. It will write your exam papers, do your resume, write a reference letter better than you can. We are relinquishing our hard-fought intelligence to something we have little control over. I asked a friend of mine to write a letter of recommendation for me for a volunteer program. She wrote a beautiful letter of reference. I asked her how she wrote such a beautiful letter. She answered,

"ChatGPT." It was the nicest letter anyone had ever written about me.

Back to the toddler in the park who so badly wanted his mom's attention. Being seen and heard is important. I waved at him and gave him a thumbs up just to let him know that I saw him, even though he had no idea who I was.

Did I really say that?

There comes a moment in everyone's life (at least I hope I am not the only one) when something comes out of our mouth that we immediately wish we could take back. Like when you ask someone you haven't seen in a long time how their husband is, even though you were at the funeral some months back. A sudden lapse of judgment or memory, or what some call a senior moment. We all have them. One of my most memorable of these moments (though I'm hoping to forget) took place at an event in Montreal. I wanted the floor to open up and swallow me whole.

I was working for a Fortune 500 company and the CEO wanted me along on a speaking engagement where we were giving out long-term service awards. As we flew from Toronto to Montreal, he reread his speech and practised people's names to get them right during the awards ceremony (English was not his first language). This was the man who used to say, "If we need to know what people think, hold a fucus group." While that was worth a chuckle, the faux pas I would later make was not.

We arrived in plenty of time. Employees from the Montreal office gathered together, some speaking French, some English, and one fluent in Italian. I, on the other hand, proceeded to make a fool of myself in English, which may have saved me.

At the reception following the awards, I approached a woman who looked very pregnant. (Note to self: Do not believe anyone is pregnant until they tell you so.) I asked her when she was due, and not missing a beat, she pretended I had not made that colossal blunder and said, in her heavily accented English, "Oh, I just got my five-year pin last year, so I am not due for another five years."

After blushing to the roots of my hair and beyond, I beat a hasty retreat. I never forgot that day. And I will never inquire about someone being pregnant. It turned out she was just a very large woman. When I think of that day, I still want the floor to swallow me whole. A perfect lesson in "open mouth, put foot in." Never again.

The flight home was very quiet. Thankfully, the big boss had no idea how empathetic I now was with his minor blunders in pronouncing people's names. As someone once said, "When you see someone struggling in English, it is because they speak more than one language," which is more than can be said of me. As the head of public relations, I was supposed to be the epitome of tact and diplomacy. I'll get right on that.

Then there was the case of "open mouth, change feet!" when I inadvertently responded on Facebook to a friend who sent a picture of himself and his wife. We had met on a cruise many years ago. He was always white haired and quite dashing, and his wife, last time I saw her, was blonde. Now, there he sat at dinner, overlooking the ocean on another cruise.

I didn't realize my eyesight was going. I should have opened up the picture to full size. Instead, I sent back a note saying, "Where are the wives?"

"That's Marnie!" was Al's immediate reply. Oops. Had I looked closer I would have seen that what I thought was a man in a black suit was really Marnie in a black dress with tiny flowers on it and her hair pulled back from her face. I had already determined that she was a man and that maybe the two men were having dinner because their wives had had high tea on the ship earlier.

How does one extricate oneself from a stupid comment? I sent back another response blaming my eyesight. Ah, the joys of aging! When will I learn to keep my mouth shut?

What goes around comes around

The older I get, the more I realize there are no coincidences. I'm not sure if there is a divine plan—a master chess player moving the pieces around—but what are the chances that a story told in university has its punch line some thirty-five years later?

I was attending my fourth year of university in London, Ontario, when a classmate and I were chatting about her first job. She was from Vancouver, but for a time she lived in Toronto, where she worked as a waitress, as they were called in those days, at a restaurant aptly named the Spaghetti House. In hindsight, considering all we had been through since the outbreak of the pandemic, her story was particularly striking.

Seems her boss at the restaurant thought milk looked better with bubbles in it, so he had all his staff blow bubbles through a straw before serving milk to the diners. Hearing this tale as we sat waiting for our psychology professor to show up for class, I thought that was pretty funny. We shared all kinds of stories as we got to know our classmates but, for some reason, this was one I never forgot.

Fast forward some thirty-five years to when my husband introduced me to his cousin in California. She was married to a very funny guy who loved to laugh and joke around. He was a lot of fun and everyone adored him. He had worked all kinds of different jobs over his life, but one day we got to talking about the Spaghetti House. He piped up, "I opened those restaurants in Canada back in the day."

"Really?" I exclaimed. "I had a friend a long time ago and she told me this bizarre story about some joker she worked for. He insisted that she blow bubbles into milk before serving it." He looked at me with a huge smile and proclaimed, "That was me!"

I thought, "What are the chances a story that started when I was a student would end so many years later?" I also wondered, "What were you thinking?!" Clearly, he wasn't, though that thought only came after growing up, becoming a mom, and knowing how easily germs spread—and after having survived Covid.

The point is, you might think a story is over, but who knows when you'll really hear the end of it? Maybe I should file things away in my brain, just in case the missing piece shows up years later. I guess that is the beauty of living a long life. You never know when the story truly ends. You just have to stick around long enough, with memory intact, to find out.

I wonder how many other stories that began long ago are still awaiting their endings?

The real end of the story

I had the good fortune to be in Israel on my nineteenth birthday. My aunt had gotten up at five in the morning to make a chocolate cake. In those days, the country was still developing and it had very little, let alone luxuries like chocolate cake. That was a special treat. In fact, any kind of chocolate had to be hunted down. Hot countries don't make all things chocolate, as I have discovered in my travels. It melts too quickly.

On this occasion, my aunt wanted to make something special for me. She was up and baking at 5 a.m. because it would be too hot later in the day. When I arrived at the breakfast table, there was this magnificent cake with the middle of the round creation cut out just for me. My aunt explained that it was the best piece of all and as the birthday girl it was mine. Heaven.

I have many memories of my trips to Israel. My aunt was always a part of them, until she passed away in her nineties.

An old saying reminds us that "time heals all things." I believe that time explains all things. In my first book, one of my stories was about how my family ended up in Israel—well, at least part of my family did. I always thought that in our small community, my dad's older sister could not find anyone "frum" (religious) enough for her liking. And so, she went off to Israel to find someone more observant than anyone in our small town.

My aunt was a mine of information about our family history. She told me how, growing up in what was then Byelorussia, she was afraid to go out into the fields where her older brother was working to bring him his lunch. She was only six years old. To his dying day, my uncle complained how hungry he was. It was only after he had passed that I learned the real story. My aunt, who had always been petite, was terrified of the crows and she was too scared to bring my uncle's lunch to him. He never knew.

In a similar fashion, on my last trip to Israel I was telling my husband that my aunt moved there to find a match who would be observant. In fact, she did end up marrying a rabbi's son. However, my cousin, their daughter, who overheard our conversation, started to laugh. "What's so funny?" I wanted to know. Cousin Tzippy explained that that was not the real reason.

Apparently, my aunt did not want to marry anyone unless they were refined, cultured and, most of all, did not eat with their fingers. Who knew? All those years of tearing old newsprint for toilet paper before shabbat came in on Friday night. Not turning on lights at her home, not going out on Saturday. All those naps to pass the time. I thought she was uber religious. Now I find out all these years later, and after she is long gone, that she moved to Israel because she thought there was no one in our small town with the manners, culture and deportment that she wanted in a spouse. What an eye opener.

There's a wonderful line from a movie about how things always work out in the end of a good story, and if they don't, then it isn't the end. I love that concept. I don't want the story to ever end. All kinds of wonderful things happen when you least expect them and surprise endings are the best of all. I hope I live long enough to enjoy many surprise happy endings. And for my aunt, wherever she is, I hope she is thrilled with how accomplished and well mannered her great-grandchildren are. They are a delight and I can't wait to go back and spend more time with them.

The Good Samaritan

My husband and I were bitten by the gardening bug shortly after I retired, and we have been working on our gardens for a number of years now. The previous owners had lots of boxwoods and last year I noticed they were not doing so well. I dutifully went off to the garden centre and purchased the solution they recommended.

Lo and behold, this year we seemed to be the only ones in the 'hood with thriving boxwoods. We were pretty excited; we are amateurs, after all. I have friends whose gardens could have come straight out of the pages of *House and Garden*. Apparently, this is a skill that gets handed down from one generation to another. I definitely did not inherit the gardening gene, but I am not afraid to ask questions or follow a schematic from a magazine. My husband is a more natural gardener and plants flowers that provide colour and variety in height and size all summer long. So, he does the perennials, I do the annuals.

One morning, my neighbour and I were exchanging fence parts. The latticework from our aging fence had fallen into their yard, thanks to an unruly lilac bush, and she was handing it back over. We were chatting when Sarah said to me that she was off to the store to get something with which to treat the boxwoods. Being the helpful neighbour I aspire to be, I told her not to bother. Not only did I know just the solution, I had enough of it for both of us and I would go get her mine, which I had already mixed into a spray bottle, saving her the trouble.

No sooner had I returned with the goods, when I climbed into our raised garden, tripped on a rock that had no business being there and face planted into my very own boxwood bush. I promise that is not the treatment to try. Sarah immediately panicked but could do nothing to help from the other side of the fence. The only thing really bruised was my vanity. How inelegant. How uncoordinated. How ridiculous I must have looked catapulting into the very plant I was trying to show her how to save. Graceful I was not. Humiliated, maybe, as I struggled to right myself and my dignity.

Sarah was concerned that I might be hurt, but I bravely told her, "I'm a skier. I am used to falling." However, it was early July, and this was not a ski hill. And in spite of believing that I am not only young at heart, but still somewhat coordinated—at least enough to hand something across a fence—it was not my day.

I do my best to be a good neighbour but, honestly, my dignity took quite the beating that day. I could just hear the boxwood bush as it muttered, "Big help you are. Why not kill me while you're at it." What I should have said to my neighbour was, "Here's the name of the solution. Good luck with your boxwoods."

Better late than never

A dear friend told me that funerals are sad because they bring back everything we feel about losses in our own families. I was at a friend's mother's funeral when I began to think of so many things I wish I could say to my mom. She was my worst critic and the first to remind me when my behaviour disappointed. I wanted to scream at her, "Just leave me alone," but she never would. In her eyes, I was an extension of her own being, so much a part of her that she sometimes couldn't see where she left off and I began. She often saw her offspring, especially her daughters, as her ambassadors in the world representing her worst and best traits. It didn't help that I was the spitting image of her, reminding her of her own human failings and unenviable flaws. At best, when I made her proud, she felt a warm glow inside, as if her daughter's accomplishments were her own. Letting go for moms is especially difficult. As a mom I now get it.

Our relationship was frustrating, maddening, infuriating, yet she was the first person I ran to for comfort, to kiss and make it better. It was a catch-22 for sure. How many times did I bristle under comments like, "You're not wearing that out, are you?" and the infamous "Have you put on a few pounds, dear?"

Though delivered with such sweetness, they could crush me like no other nasty comment to my face or behind my back. And when providing dating advice on my chosen beau? "You know you could do better than that." But what if I liked that? Between the "Oh, sweetheart, how could you?" and the "Don't you think you should have said . . ." I became adept at second guessing my own judgment.

Separating and individuating from my mom was something I spent a good chunk of my life doing. I suspect all daughters do. And yet, there were always the good characteristics I hoped I had inherited. My mom used to say, "You got your father's hair, you lucky thing." Never did I hear her say, "But thank goodness you did not inherit his teeth," which were always in the shop for repair, so to speak. Beyond the genetic likenesses, I also inherited strength of character.

Despite all the frustrations, I didn't know how I would ever survive without her when my mom eventually passed on; in fact, it was heartbreak of the most painful kind. What I should have said, could have said, would have said if only I'd had the chance. Once I was a mom myself, I often forgot and forgave her missteps along the parenting path as I realized just what a tough and thankless job parenting could be.

For every piece of unsolicited advice given over the years, for every "Oh, how could you?" or every time I hoped she'd say "I'm so proud of you, or "Good for you for sticking to your guns," rather than doubting my integrity, I can look back and say, "I wasn't all that bad after all, was I?" And to be fair, there was the occasional, "Aren't you clever" mixed in with the "Did you remember to write a thank-you note?"

That bond with my mom could only be fully understood when she was gone. If only I had given her credit when it was due all those years ago. Somehow, the words went unsaid until after, when it was too late. After, when I realized she was right all along about so many things. When I so wished I had one more chance to sit with her, laugh with her and share my daily ups and downs. When I realized that, despite many frustrations, she was a very wise and influential mom. The older I get, the wiser she becomes. Sad but true that I only gave my mom her due long after she was gone. I guess better late than never.

I wish . . . I could be good enough

The question "Am I good enough?" must have engraved itself on my brain in childhood. It catches me by surprise at the oddest moments. I had friends over for brunch on Sunday and was worried about using paper plates in the backyard. So often when we have company for dinner, I stress over the food, the tableware, who to seat next to whom. A friend reminds me that friends and family don't come for the food, they come to be together. And after a year of losing good friends and family members, I am feeling how important being together really is.

Tomorrow I am having some women in for lunch. One friend is going away for five weeks and I thought it would be nice to have a little get-together in her honour. I remember a friend of my late mother's, who outlived her by about twelve years, telling the story of how they became friends. My mom, who lived in the same complex, had lost her husband, my father, a short time before. This woman, Barbara, had also recently lost her husband. They met in the elevator and my mom, being the hospitable person she was, invited Barbara to join her for lunch, as she was having some people in. Barbara insisted that she had a hair appointment and could not make it, but my mom persevered and invited her to come by after the appointment, which Barbara did. They became lifelong friends.

This story was running through my head as I was trying to decide if I should include a friend who had recently lost her son in my own little get-together. Would she want to come? Was she feeling like being social? Should I even ask? And then I remembered the story Barbara told long after my mom had passed. So, I invited her. We have already been lifelong friends. We've been through a lot together. And we have always been there for one another, so why not now?

Then began my stressing. Would the food be good enough? Everyone was chipping in and bringing a dish, but there I was hearing the old voice in my head. Of course, the solution was to spend all day in the kitchen baking and cooking and running around like a chicken with my head cut off. Being busy would surely bring the desired result. This same feeling creeps in when I wonder if I will sell any books. Are they good enough?

Bottom line is, am I good enough?

My friends are not interested in the food or décor. They just want to be together.

Maybe it's the getting together itself that worries me. Maybe I would rather be on my own and not entertain at all. I do like to cook and entertain in small doses, but this week it's one brunch after a lunch before a dinner for eight. Who does this to themselves? Will our company for dinner be okay with hotdogs and hamburgers? It's a barbecue, for heaven's sake. They are not expecting a fancy ball, although I have put on plenty of major dinners for occasions and holidays. They know I can cook. I know I can cook—and yet I wonder if it will be good enough.

I should be an old pro at this point in my life, but I always feel that niggling doubt.

It's quite the conundrum to me how one acquires the self-confidence and belief in oneself that it's all okay. There used to be a book entitled *I'm OK-You're OK*. And okay is good enough. My version of the book is *You're Okay, I'm Not So Hot*. Where did I learn this?

How do we instill confidence in our kids and grandkids without giving them big heads or false confidence? Unearned bravado is just as dangerous as constantly wondering if we are enough. It's not like I go around asking for reassurance. I just torture myself in silence. I should feel accomplished by now. I did well academically and had a career I absolutely adored, which I understand now is a rarity. I'm pretty good at getting back up after I have been knocked down and I feel pretty good about most of the decisions I have made for myself. I hope I make a difference in other people's lives. And yet . . . when do we ever feel good enough?

Back to my lunch: I have had years of practice in the kitchen and entertaining. What am I worried about? So I just plunge in. "Feel the fear and do it anyway," they say. Of course, when it is all over, I am usually pleased with the result and feel like I have accomplished something. That need to achieve is still deeply ingrained in me from childhood, a legacy from my parents for sure. Just like caring for others is. Yet, I still wonder why I can't just say to myself, "Self, you are good enough just as you are. Now go out there and enjoy."

Perhaps I am like everyone else seeking to define and redefine myself from one decade to another. I guess it is a lifelong process. Maybe at the end I will feel I have been good enough. And if I don't, as that character in that movie once said, "Then it is not the end."

I suspect I am not alone in these thoughts. I wish I could say to myself again and again, "You are good enough. Stop working so hard at it. You don't need to be the best at anything. You are out there trying new things and doing your best. You are good enough just as you are."

A look on the bright side

My husband and I were out biking and all was going well. Until it wasn't. I could see Jay fall off his bike in slow motion, landing hard on his bad hip. Uh-oh. Was it a sympathy fall when I encountered the same spot and ended up down on the ground on my own hip?

What is it with getting older? My balance may not be as good as it was when I was ten years old (although I do remember taking some bad tumbles over my handlebars then too). Here I was, sixty some years later, in a panic, asking if Jay was okay. Did he fall on the bad hip? Yes. Did he hurt himself? Well, no, because he is a macho man deep down inside and men don't cry. But I bet he wanted to.

The irony was that I fell on my right side, and I am right-handed. He fell on his left and is left-handed, and both of us had identical road rash injuries on our elbows. A matched pair! A matched pair of klutzes.

Never mind. We got back on our bikes and continued on our way. Until on the return trip I did something stupid (aren't all accidents stupid?) and went ass-over-teakettle over a curb. I used to be able to bike down curbs quite fine if the momentum was right. Not on this bike, which I suddenly realized was bigger than I can now handle. Heavy sigh, and off to Emergency, limping all the way.

I was grateful that hubby has privileges at the hospital, and after forty-eight years on staff had earned us VIP treatment. In came the doctor with my x-ray results. I had a hairline fracture of my tibial plateau. While hubby was absorbing the news, he missed what came next: "What does this mean in lay language?" I asked. "You have a busted knee," came the answer. I think I liked it better when I didn't understand. And I am a doctor's daughter and a doctor's wife who worked in health care for years.

On the bright side, it could have been a lot worse, we were told. Yes, indeed. Next came the orthopedic resident. I tried hard not to think he was soooo young. "As long as he knows his stuff," I told myself. He was warm and friendly and very knowledgeable. I liked him even better when he said no surgery, no cast (though he did not say no pain). Just an orthopedic splint for the foreseeable future. I could even do a bit of walking. He checked his diagnosis with the lead orthopedic surgeon (who happened to be the one operating on my hubby's hip a few months later), and he was correct. However, no biking, no golfing and no swimming either. Hmm. I still liked him, and as it turned out, he lived in our neighbourhood. Go figure. It is a very small world, a world of which, I realized, I am on the way out (though eventually, not immediately), and this young doctor is the future. Thankfully, he had us out of there in no time.

While disappointed that my summer plans were now on holiday, I felt huge gratitude for the kindness and skill of the doctors and techs. The X-ray technician and I had worked at the same hospital many years ago. He had come out of retirement to work at this hospital part time. We shared stories of people we knew and talked retirement and how important it is to stay active and involved. It is easy to gripe about how systems are falling apart, including our health care system, but everyone was so professional and so good to me. I felt pretty damned thankful and blessed for the care I got, not to mention for having the good sense to marry my husband when I did.

We will get right back on the bikes again. Maybe I will trade mine in for a lighter one, but I will ignore my friends who say, "Forget biking. You're too old for that." My response is, you are never too old for stupidity, which was the cause, I confess, of both falls.

Besides, for the past eleven months, I have shouldered most of the household chores. It can't be a coincidence that, come this Tuesday, my hubby finishes saying prayers twice a day for his dad, who passed away last year. That means he will have time to do the things I can't, like walk our dog and do all the errands while I take it easy for the next four weeks of healing. Funny about the timing.

Learning to say yes

I have asked it before and I will ask it again: Why is it so hard to accept help from others?

Is it just me or are we all like that? When you are incapacitated, yet you insist you can do it all yourself, there is definitely something wrong with your thought process. Do only women suffer from this, or do men deal with it too? Who told us we had to do it all ourselves?

I suspect our three-year-old selves are coming back to haunt us. "I do it my own self!" Note the exclamation point. Every three-year-old, including our granddaughter, speaks in exclamation points, and with the confidence we wish we could hold onto our entire lives.

Since I have been laid up (or sabotaged by my bicycle, that traitor), I have received so many offers of help from kind friends. "Can I pick up groceries?" "Can I take you somewhere?" "What do you need?" Now, there's a loaded question. How about a new knee or a faster recovery?

But then, we must all count our blessings and be grateful for small favours. Yes, I am grateful for the good care I received in Emerg. Yes, I am very happy it wasn't worse. Yes, I do not need surgery, and yes, I appreciate that my splint is removable. But, damn it, I want to be active and keep moving.

It is not in my nature to say yes when friends ask if they can help. I have determination and stubbornness in spades and would like to get on with my life. Trouble is, I can't.

Turns out this is a great lesson in not doing everything myself. I am practising saying yes for a change. Yes, you can pick up eggs for me. So what if they are extra-large and I only buy large? Yes, some groceries would be lovely. Okay, it's a new pasta I have never tried before. Who cares? In the grand scheme of things, what does it matter? And yes, you can go to the basement and bring up what I need from storage since I can't do the stairs.

This business of saying yes is a weird, foreign feeling, but I am going to keep trying.

Learning to embrace what is, is a huge challenge. Life can be downright cruel at its worst, and challenging on any average day. So many frustrations, like bad customer service, thoughtless drivers and people wrapped up in their own lives instead of paying attention to ours.

Being ill or laid up is our chance to embrace where we are and accept what our friends offer. There is, after all, a bright side to everything, so I'm told. I just need to learn to lean back and relax and say "yes" in spite of the fact that my first instinct is to say, "No thanks, I'm fine (I can do it my own self!)." I don't need to prove myself anymore. As I like to say, I have less time ahead of me than I do behind me.

What's wrong with needing help? It is not evidence that I am incapable, but rather of the number of friends I have, even if only one is offering help at any one time. And it feels good to help someone in need does it not? Why deny someone else the opportunity to feel good by helping me? Then there is the whole concept of patience, as I was reminded by a dear friend who was struck by a car last year and needed many months to recuperate. She has a point. The patient must be patient. Oh, to be a Buddhist right now.

Speaking of mindfulness, even though I am technically allowed to drive, I have lost all confidence that I should. I bet the insurance company would agree. Driving with the right leg while the left is injured is probably not the best idea, as I discovered while sailing past the drive-through window for a coffee, blithely forgetting to stop and order, and ending up at the pickup window.

"You must be constantly mindful," my experienced friend remonstrated. "Not just driving, but even contemplating which foot to use first on the stairs." That's a whole other subconscious split-second decision that now requires concentrated effort at the top and bottom of the stairs. Bad leg first, going down. Good leg first, going up. Who remembers these things? I try to remember: "Bad, Bad Leroy Brown, baddest man in the whole damned town." And for the good leg, "Good Golly Miss Molly . . ." I have always been too busy for mindfulness, but now it might be a matter of life and death.

In answer to the question I started with, it's been reassuring to learn that I am not the only one who hates to ask for help.

I have also learned that the best way to offer help is to be specific and timely. "I am free this afternoon around 2 p.m., can I take you to the bank?" is so much better than, "Call me if you need anything, I am here for you." My dog is here for me too, but big help she is.

So I have learned a lot. To be a good friend you can make a dinner. Just double what you are making for yourself. No real extra effort involved. In the future, if and when I am mobile again, when I want to be helpful and I am going shopping, I will call and say, "I am going to do groceries. Please text me your list and I will drop your stuff off." I'm working on it so I can be a better friend next time.

But first, I have six more weeks in this splint. I'm still going to get my meat order for the High Holidays delivered and cook when no one is watching. I can only behave for so long.

When the rabbi calls

It was Friday night, about sundown mid-summer. We were just about to put dinner on the barbecue when the phone rang. It was the rabbi. Jay had just finished eleven months of morning and evening prayers. We thought it was behind us. "We are short for a minyan (minimum ten men required for davening [prayers]). Can you come?" We live in the neighbourhood and as I motioned to my husband, "Go, go," I heard him respond, "It will take me six minutes to get there." And off he went.

It seemed to me like the right thing to do. I was all for it. I had spent a huge part of the day in Emerg at the hospital learning that the knee I fractured was still fractured, no surprise, and that I would be another five weeks, minimum, in a splint. I was disappointed. It's frustrating when something like a fractured body part puts you out of commission. No golf. No swimming. No biking (the culprit). My thinking was that, despite my frustration and feeling quite down, I had best say yes if God was calling.

Okay, it wasn't really God, but pretty darned close. After all, who says no to a rabbi? And I like this rabbi, and the other ones too, at this Chabad sanctuary. They were good to my husband

and he had developed quite a fondness for the community. How could you not? Morning and night you are rearranging your schedule for almost a year and making up a very small group of devoted men who are committed to praying twice a day. You can't help but make friends.

And so it was with a sigh of relief (on Jay's part) that I did not object, and within two seconds I was barbecuing on one leg and he was off and running to shul (synagogue) to make up the minyan, as without a tenth man you can't pray (well, you can if your synagogue is reform or even modern conservative, but definitely not Chabad, which is very traditional in its practices). It wasn't that I was being magnanimous. In fact, I was hedging my bets. Maybe if I was agreeable and sent the needed tenth man along, God might remember that and speed up the healing of my knee, without which, I confess, I can't do much.

Besides, this is a congregation I like very much, as it reminds me of home. The first time I attended services there it felt like the small-town synagogue of my childhood, with sixty Jewish families and one very sweet rabbi. One sanctuary had to serve all levels of the Jewish faith. The way it was designed, the very religious men sat on one side of the bimah (raised platform where the Ark sits), the very religious or Orthodox women sat on the other side of the bimah, and in the middle sat those who were more Conservative, men and women together. Then there were the children who sprinkled themselves throughout as they chose, as well as up in the balcony far from parental eyes, but not ears, where chaos reigned. The beauty of this small community was that, when we were in the building, kids like me did not have to report in to our parents. Everyone looked out for everyone else's kids and that made it a very tight community. The Chabad synagogue is like that. Everyone knows everyone and when you attend you get added in to the mix. It is a caring community—a microcosm of a much greater society. I love that feeling.

This community is what got Jay through the last year of mourning and praying and it's what made me say "Go" the very instant the rabbi called. I may not be up to dancing right now, but this I can do.

My Israeli family

Since October 7, 2023, Israel has been in the news constantly. For some of us it is also in our hearts and prayers every day of our lives, not just on October 7. For those of us with family there, our thoughts are constantly with them. I have always felt a special bond with my Israeli family. Every Thursday I call my cousin Tzippy (short for Tzipora, which in Hebrew means bird). We have been close my whole life even though there are about fifteen years and a number of oceans separating us. How does this happen?

My father was the youngest of five. And I was the youngest of the next generation. The bad news was that, come Passover, I was always the nervous youngster who had to ask the Four Questions at the family seder. All of my cousins were about fifteen to twenty-five years older than I, but Tzippy and I were especially close. Every time I went to Israel she was there for me.

At sixteen, when my parents thought I should spend a summer there on a youth program and I was terribly homesick after having almost lost my father several times during the previous months, she rescued me. I stupidly thought I would wake up in time to take a bus from Jerusalem to where they lived in Petach Tikvah. By the time I woke up that bus was long gone. Who knew when the next one would be? I don't remember how I got myself to the station. It was a foreign country where people only spoke Hebrew. I knew nothing of how to get around, never mind to the bus station. I do remember that there was no way to let Tzippy know I had missed the bus. Back then, in 1969, there were no cell phones and very few pay phones, and the ones there were required a special token.

Tzippy met every single bus from Jerusalem arriving in Petach Tikva all day long. And she was more than nine months pregnant with her second boy. I was there when he was born. I met her first son, who was about eighteen months old at the time. Later, she would have a third son. I have been close to all of them for over fifty-five years. They age. I don't. (Wink).

This past year, David, her wonderful husband passed away. I miss him so much. He was the one who drove us everywhere. I would get off a plane in the middle of the night. He was there to meet me. Jetlagged and barely keeping my eyes open, he would take us to Jaffa for dinner at ten o'clock in the evening. Did I ever tell him how much I loved him? Do we ever tell our family how much they mean to us? Of course we tell our children, but what about older relatives who have made a huge difference in our lives?

My mother would send clothes for the family, as they had so little. Everyone there had very little. On that trip back in 1969, I brought Cousin David a yellow golf shirt that my mom had picked out for him. Every time I visited him that summer over the course of eight weeks, he was wearing the yellow shirt.

I loved him for it. It meant my gift (or my mom's) meant a lot to him.

Over time, my cousins no longer needed these gifts. Their country grew into one of the most sophisticated and fashion-forward in the world, right before my eyes. Over the many years I have been visiting Israel I have been astounded at the leaps and bounds the country has made since my first trip. From a country that was constantly being attacked on all sides, with war-torn roads, leftover tanks and rubble, to this incredibly modern and sophisticated country on par with any of the most technologically advanced in the world. How did they do this? Every time I visited, there was a new glass tower in the skyline of Tel Aviv.

Today the fashion is second to none in design and creativity. The art, the culture, the music and dance too. I am amazed how accomplished my own cousins' children are. A talented dancer. A concert pianist at the age of fourteen. A brilliant photographer. A gifted athlete. And all of them extremely bright. There are so many universities. Perhaps their great-grandparents, who were also mine and whose mantra was education, education, education, are looking down proudly at them. Don't just sit there, read a book. Learn something. Better yourself. My parents' words follow me today. Their universal words about lifting ourselves up to be something better are the backbone of Israel's success. It boggles the mind.

Back to my cousin and her late husband. Why is it so hard to tell the people we love most that they have made a huge difference in our lives? Why can't we tell them when they are alive? I will miss David's wisdom, his kindness, his quirky sense of humour, his love of family. All of his children have a love of their country and its natural beauty. They inherited his passion for hiking, for traveling, for learning and for seeing as much of the world as possible. His kindness and curiosity along with a great sense of humour are built into his boys, my cousins. They take turns staying overnight with their mom so she won't be alone. I reassure her that they are his legacy (and hers). She is devastated by her loss. We all are. I will always remember him in my heart and be grateful for what a wonderful human being he was. For his surviving family, I hope for peace in their hearts and peace in their land, which they have all fought so hard to keep secure.

The cane mutiny

This year marked ten years since our last trip to Israel. It was high time to go. However, our attempts to get there were constantly thwarted over the year. The war that began on October 7, 2023, played havoc with our plans, as had my unwell father-in-law prior to that. We kept delaying our trip and finally got there in 2024. We had heard about volunteer opportunities and chose one for the first five days. Many of us stayed at a hotel in Tel Aviv before and after the volunteering stint.

The hotel took very good care of us, fed us breakfast every day and snacks throughout the day. In the evening there was soup, wine and more snacks, which were very welcome indeed. Because most of the guests had volunteered all day, we would sit together and share stories of our experiences, folding uniforms, picking fruit and vegetables and filling in where workers would normally be if they were not in the army. It was all hands on deck, so to speak.

One evening I noticed a woman playing the piano in the lobby. She played beautifully and I told her so. Juanita delighted in telling us her story. Seems she was born in the Caribbean and married someone Jewish. It turned out that this very unassuming woman was a concert pianist who had moved to Israel from

New York. Her husband had since passed away, so she made her home at the hotel, moving her piano there with her.

Juanita would sit down and perform the most beautiful music, then disappear for the evening, returning all dolled up having just performed a concert at one of the many concert halls. Remarkable. Did I mention she told me she was well into her nineties? When I asked where she learned to play, she answered one word: "Practice." Her mother insisted she learn to play the piano and she has been practising all her life. The other noticeable feature of this very talented woman was that she was speaking fluent Hebrew. Did I mention she was Black, and had lived in Jamaica and the southern U.S., then New York City, before moving to Israel?

We enjoyed chatting with Jaunita. She especially liked my husband's walking cane. Yes, he was headed for another hip surgery in the coming year, though it didn't stop him from working all day as a volunteer and touring the country and golfing at the only eighteen-hole golf course in the country. When Juanita remarked at how lovely the butterflies were on his cane, comparing it to her plain brown one, I offered to send her one from back home. She was amazed that I would do that for her.

Of course I would.

Sometime later in the month when we were back home, I remembered my promise, so off I went to find the same cane with the butterflies, like the one my husband uses. Some half dozen drug stores later, and nowhere near where we lived, I found it. The drugstore also had a post office, so I figured I would bubble wrap it, address it and send it along. The price to mail the cane to Israel was exorbitant, but a promise is a promise.

A few weeks later an acquaintance mentioned she was going to Israel to volunteer with her daughter, and she happened to be staying at the same hotel. I asked her to look for Jaunita and to tell her that her cane was on its way. Then I forgot all about it.

Three months later, a FedEx truck arrived at our house and left the very same package with the cane at our front door. "What is this?" I thought. "Didn't I mail you away a few months ago? What are you doing back here? Is this the cane mutiny? Why are you here on my doorstep and not with Juanita?"

I had paid more than $100 to send a $35 cane overseas and it came back to me? The package was addressed properly: Jaunita the Piano Player, Maxim Hotel, Tel Aviv, with all the details. It was covered in Israeli stickers I did not understand, but in English it said, "Unclaimed." What happened? Did they not leave it with the front desk? After all, Juanita lived in the hotel. Perhaps she was no longer alive. That would make me very sad. I vowed to call the hotel and find out what happened.

In telling this story to a friend who was leaving for Israel the next day and whom I secretly hoped would offer to deliver the cane, she said, "Are you crazy? Who does that? Who pays almost $100 to ship a $35 cane? You don't think the drugstores in Israel carry canes? Don't tell anyone this story." I even asked her directly if she would take the cane to the hotel when she was there. "Not a chance," said she. "It doesn't fit in my luggage and I have too many bags to begin with."

I remained defiant. I was once told I was tenacious. I had to look the word up in the dictionary because I had no idea what it meant. Just give me a challenge, like a returned cane thwarting my desire to be a good citizen, and watch how tenacious I can be. It is a beautiful cane, and I know for a fact, because I called, that the Israeli drugstore near the hotel does not carry this type of cane. I felt it was a small price to pay for all the enchanting music Jaunita provided, not to mention how warm and friendly she was.

First, I had to find out if Jaunita was still at her piano. I called the hotel and spoke with her directly. "Juanita, it's Marjie from Canada. I'm the one who said I would get you the pretty butterfly cane." She remembered me. I told her I that I had sent it, but it never reached her. She was so annoyed that the staff of the hotel never told her it had arrived. In their defense, it might not have left the post office in Israel, but surely someone would have tried to reach her. No, she had not moved and had no plans to do so. Yes, she was still playing the piano. I promised I would get the cane to her if I had to bring it myself. She told me she knew I was a good person and that people like me restore her faith in humanity, though she wasn't so impressed with the post office.

Now what to do? Send it again for another $100 or fly to Israel and deliver it in person? I was still pondering that when I spoke with the owner of the hotel. He told me there was always someone coming from Toronto, and I should send it with them.

Then I remembered our "women in the tent"; we had created a chat group after our volunteer experience in Israel. We even had a reunion in June. It was now almost September, but I put out an all-points bulletin to ask if anyone could help me carry out this mitzvah (good deed). Sure enough, one very kind soul said she was heading to Israel at the end of October. I asked if she minded taking a bigger suitcase or if she might want to use the cane on the journey. She had injured herself moving some appliances around earlier that day, and thought she might just do that. And she would be staying at the same hotel.

I was thrilled that the cane would be on its way to the intended owner and hoped there would be no more mutinies, either by the cane or the post office.

Birds of a feather

When we traveled to Israel in the spring of 2024, I wanted to buy a piece of art as a souvenir. Not just any piece of art, but one significant painting that would grace the wall in our living room or den. Over the years we had collected many beautiful renderings of Jerusalem and we have some well-known artists' work. This time I wanted something created by an Israeli artist that was not a street scene or a cityscape, something unique and special.

It poured rain during our time in Caesarea, where the ancient Roman ruins are. We visited the little shops and art galleries in town. On the wall in one gallery were magnificent renderings of brilliantly coloured birds done in fabric, one thread at a time, something I had not seen before. I asked the shop manager about the different pieces, all of which would be too large to take with us. She assured us they could ship to Canada.

We took pictures of our favourites and went on with our day, but one particular rendering kept returning to me. It was a modernistic picture of different-coloured birds, some pink and blue, some orange, some green, some purple, perched in the branches of trees against a grey background in light and dark tones. Set against this foreboding backdrop, the joyous birds reminded me that, in spite of tragedy, in spite of unspeakable loss, there is always beauty, and the birds will always sing. Now, maybe I was reading way too much into this artwork, but it spoke to me and it was created by an Israeli.

When we got home, we got in touch with the art dealer. Yes, they still had the piece we had admired. Yes, they could ship it to us. At that point I began my research into the man who created this work. As it turned out, he was born in Montreal. He was identified as a rising young talent at the age of eight, and at some point he moved to Israel to study with a renowned artist who taught him this method of creating images out of silk thread. How ironic! I wanted an Israeli artist and ended up with a work created by someone born in Montreal. A fellow Canadian. The artist had passed away just two years before we saw his work in the gallery, but he had been commissioned by some of Israel's major public spaces and cultural halls, where his work now hangs.

When I mentioned the artist's name to my cousin Tzippy (which, you may recall, means "bird" in Hebrew), she said that our mutual first cousin from Toronto had dated someone with the same name from Montreal. In fact, she had come with him to Israel and introduced him to Tzippy. Turns out, this man was the right age to have been the brother of the artist's father, who lived in Montreal and who also recently passed away. Cousin Tzippy met the artist's uncle when he and Cousin Sandy were in Israel. Visiting his artist nephew, perhaps? It was a long time ago now, and Cousin Sandy has been gone for fifteen years, so we don't know for sure (but they say there is no such thing as coincidence).

Now this lovely creation hangs on our living room wall. The birds have come to our home to roost. If they are symbolic of anything, they may be telling us to flock together in good times and bad, and to hang tough. We will get through this. We birds have to stick together.

One last coincidence: Tzippy's grandson is a very accomplished photographer and takes wonderful pictures of birds, which he now sends me on a regular basis.

An eye-opening visit

There are many countries in the world where those in their senior years are respected and revered. I had a chance to experience this firsthand on a trip to Vietnam. I was part of a Habitat for Humanity Global Village build that took place before Covid, about 2014. Twelve of us Canadians from all across the country packed our duffle bags and headed to Saigon, or Ho Chi Minh City, as it is now called.

Our mission was to build two homes south of a village in the Mekong Delta. The heat was incredible. As we boated down the Mekong River, we could almost hear the rotors of the American helicopters during the Vietnam War in the Sixties, a war the Vietnamese call the American War.

We were headed to a small village where the Communist government along with local social workers had chosen two families badly in need of better housing. On the site where we were to build, the family was living in a corrugated shack that was open front and back, with ducks and chickens wandering in and out. The kitchen, I assume due to the relentless sweltering humidity, was out back of the house. With no running water inside the home, there was an outhouse and a tap out back with a washing machine hooked up, though the machine got repossessed when the monthly installments ran out. The average household in Vietnam had beds made out of wood, with no mattresses. There was, however, a television.

As guests of the Communist government, our lodgings were a little better. Some days we had hot water, some days a bar of soap, and occasionally a towel. We'd learned from past experience to bring our own soap and towels.

Back to our family for whom we were building a home. The grandfather and grandmother were about ten years younger than I. The grandmother looked after their daughter's baby, who napped in a hammock. The baby's mom worked in a Saigon hotel as a maid during the week, coming home on weekends.

Grandfather was on the building site all day with the engineer. The family provided the sweat equity and we were the hired help (really, volunteers). Our funding helped purchase the building materials. When it was time to mix the mortar—made of sand, water and cement powder—the formula was written in chalk on the wall. It was all very rustic and basic, but it worked.

Of the twelve people on the trip, I was probably the oldest. The young'uns, as I called them, would compete to see who could carry the most bricks. I just took my ten each trip and brought them back to the building site. The concrete flooring went in first, then we bricklayers started on the walls. On most other builds there was no discussion about how old anyone was, but I got the distinct impression from the younger crew that they thought I was pretty much over the hill. One day, I asked one of the youngsters, in her early thirties, why she was pushing so hard to compete. This was not my first build with Habitat, so

I knew it was not usually a competitive sport. Her response was, "I don't want to wake up one day and be a fat, unfit sixty-year-old." I was dumbstruck.

There were all kinds of nasty things I wished I'd said. To whom was she referring, I wondered. Is that how I appeared to this young chick? The old hen was not amused, and, for the record, I still have plenty of tricks up my sleeve.

In contrast, the Vietnamese loved me, and the fact that I was older but still volunteering delighted them. They couldn't do enough for me. Needless to say, I hung out with them and not the nasty piece of work on our team.

The liaison from Habitat Vietnam was on site every day, and every so often the members of the Communist party came by on a motorcycle. Every afternoon the bahn man came by pushing his bicycle with his canteen of goods offering coffee and local delicacies, but we had been told not to eat the local street food. The community children, still wearing their uniforms, would return home to their parents, who were tending the fields of dragon fruit and minding the local ducks and geese. I put two of the kids to work with me sanding beams that were going to go up near the roof. We couldn't speak much to each other, but it was fun getting to know the family.

What was so striking to me as the senior member of the delegation was the respect shown to me. I got the pick of the jobs, one day twisting rebar, another day gathering errant wire and construction materials so we would not trip on the site. Every day the liaison would come and ask me in her smattering of English what I would like for dinner. How bizarre! She would tell me that night's dinner would be Thai food. What dishes did

I like? I thought we were making idle chitchat, but came dinner time, all the foods I said I liked were on the table. When I was working in the hot sun, the grandfather brought me a bench to sit on. I asked him if we could take the sign that said "Welcome Canadians" and tilt it so that we could work in the shade. He nodded in the 100-degree heat. No sooner had I said this than, the next day, there was this wonderful canopy covering where I was working. I could get used to this respect. Heady stuff indeed.

It never dawned on me at the time that it was because I was older than the grandparents that I got to pick the menu, get the choice worksite jobs and receive special respect from all of the Vietnamese. It was part of their culture to treat their seniors with the utmost dignity and kindness. Finally, I realized that was why they were being so deferential.

I didn't know if I should be happy or sad. Would that we could adopt some of their customs here. It seems our society has very little time for those of us who are older. I think those younger than us do not understand that we have been through everything they are going through. We just seem aged. Perhaps that is why I still colour my hair, so I can blend in a little better.

And just like these young ones now, it never dawned on me as I was growing up that seniors were so much more knowledgeable and could be a wonderful source of information and historical context. By the time this realization struck me, it was too late—I had become one of those seniors myself.

This is certainly something to think about. If it is respect I am looking for, perhaps I should go back to Vietnam.

Everyone needs a Kitchen Cabinet

Not long ago, when I was scheduled to speak at an event, a dear friend invited her real estate colleagues to join her at her table. When the day arrived, she introduced me to her colleagues saying, "This is my Real Estate Cabinet."

"Your who?" I replied.

She told me these were her most trusted colleagues who guided her through years of business issues and quandaries, adding their expertise to hers. How cool was that?

And then I remembered Golda Meir, a former prime minister of Israel who was known to have held the occasional Cabinet meeting in her kitchen and would feed her ministerial colleagues from their parliament. Historical notes refer to her Kitchen Cabinet and I began to think, I have a Kitchen Cabinet too.

If you're an "E" on the Myers-Briggs Type Indicator (a personality test) as I am, you count on trusted friends and advisers when you don't know what to do. These are the people you call on in a crisis. They are the ones who talk you down when you are about to leap from that metaphorical ledge. They often begin their advice on the state of your life with something like, "You know I love you" or "You're my dearest friend but . . ." and they go on to tell you that you are so far off the mark, you should be counting your blessings, not planning someone's demise.

We trust them with our life, but in the end, of course, we all make our own stupid decisions. Many of my friends retreat into their shell the minute there is any conflict or disruption in their lives. No amount of offering help breaks through; they are going to do what they are going to do.

Not I. No. I count on this group of trusted advisors. In other words, I have had a Kitchen Cabinet all along.

A smart person once said to me, "Don't go looking for a challah in Canadian Tire." He was so insightful. How many of us go to someone for advice on personal relationships when theirs are a mess? Who wants to ask a plumber about an electrical problem? Similarly, we can't lean on someone who has just lost their husband for advice about some silly misdemeanor our own has committed. You don't go to a friend who has not had the good fortune to have children to complain about your own. There's an innate sensitivity required here.

I think it is in the Talmud where a man complained that he had no shoes until he met the man who had no feet. Likewise, we want someone who has walked in our proverbial shoes to provide advice or talk us down from the ledge before we leap off that tall building.

Such are the benefits of the Kitchen Cabinet. In mine, I have friends who do not think exactly as I do. What would be the point? They will just tell me to go ahead and leap. In times of crisis or concern, I want the cool, calm and collected. I don't shop in Canadian Tire for a challah. Differences of opinion are good for the soul. They are good for balance in our lives and I am so grateful mine have a ton of life experience. I count on them time and again, and when they need me, I'm in their Kitchen Cabinet with expertise for them.

The family knish

Why are we so wrapped up in our own lives that we show little curiosity about our parents and their parents? Why is it that one day we wake up in our sixties or seventies and our parents are either gone or too far gone to answer our questions? And why are we much more interested in where we came from and how we came to be when we are older? Is all of this by design?

I always knew where my father's family originated. My uncle would tell me stories about the old country, as my father died first at the unexpected age of sixty-three. You would think having lost one parent young that I would immediately try to gather family lore on my mother's side. But no, I was too busy. Too wrapped up in my own world. Husband, daughter, work, school, life. Sadly, it happens.

Then one day I wondered, Who was this relative, Etta Raiza, my sister was named for? And how did half my mom's family end up in Massachusetts while all the rest ended up in South Africa? At least I was smart enough to know that these questions merited further exploration. Out of the blue a cousin called me from Chile, where she and her husband now lived. Renee wanted to know where our maternal grandparents were buried. I knew the answer, as I had taken a trip to Winthrop, Massachusetts, to visit their graves. I was smart enough before cell phone days to grab a photo of the tombstones, so I knew exactly what to tell Renee. Seems she was going to make a trip to the Boston area and I was happy I could help.

Some weeks later Renee sent a follow-up email to all of us first cousins on my mom's side. One Alan Disler lives in Los Angeles. Turns out there is another Alan Disler from South Africa living in San Diego. Renee sussed this out. Who knew? Turns out this San Diego Disler's grandfather Willie and our grandfather Kalman were brothers. Could they both be named for the same relative? And now, like me, Renee also asked the question: How did one end up in the U.S. while the other ended up in Benoni, South Africa?

I remembered my trip to South Africa and how we visited the Garden Synagogue in Cape Town. In the basement of the synagogue was a Jewish Museum, and there I found the records of who came from where. In May 1921, a family of Dislers (Yankel, sixty-five; Rosa, sixty; and their twenty-one-year-old daughter, Hanna) arrived in Cape Town on the Union Castle Line. Six years later, in January 1927, Pesse (thirty-seven) and Lijze (three) joined them. Yankel was listed as a cabinet maker. That made sense to me, as my grandfather had been head of the carpenters' union in Winthrop, Massachusetts.

I forwarded this to Renee and Cousin Alan in San Diego. Alan confirmed that it was his late grandmother for whom my sister was named. This began a wonderful communication among the cousins, and we all started sharing what few memories we had of our own grandmother. The other Alan Disler remembered her fabulous knishes. She was a caterer after all. Alan could remember their flavour and was craving them to this day. He is now in his seventies, or maybe older. Did anyone have the recipe, he wondered.

Just for fun, I pulled out my grandmother's small, black handwritten recipe book, wrapped tightly with an elastic so it would not fall apart. No knish recipe. Next, I tried my mom's recipe book, also falling apart from use and held together with an elastic. Lo and behold, what should I find in the meat section but the heading "Knishes," and the source was "Mother," which is what my mom called her mom.

There was the recipe in all its simplicity, in my mother's handwriting, no less. I was so happy to be able to send it to Cousin Alan. He instantly answered with OMG (oh my God). He can't wait to make it. True to form my mom had left out what temperature to bake them at, and for how long, but I have enough experience in the kitchen to fill in the information. I was so happy to make my cousin's wish come true. He commented in a follow-up email that he felt our grandmother was bringing the family together all these years later.

One final note. After writing my last book, *Tales from the Curio Cabinet*, about a cabinet I have whose glass door opens mysteriously in response to a *mitzvah* (good deed) my mom would have approved of, a friend commented that, when the cabinet door swings open, maybe it's not just my mom checking in on us. It might be the whole entire *mishpocha* (family). After all, they were cabinet makers. I must see if there is a signature stamp on that cabinet somewhere. You just never know!

Acknowledgements

While it's my name that ends up on the cover of the book, there are so many people who go into making the finished product.

To my early readers who were there at the beginning: Barbara Snelgrove, Eleanor Minuk and Marlene Cooper, thank you for that first read—for your wisdom and critiques and for making the book better.

To my editor, Marial Shea, you shore me up when I get discouraged. Without your insightful comments, your wit, compassion and unbelievable skill as a wordsmith, I would have chucked the whole thing in the garbage. You convinced me that I had something worth saying and that readers would identify. Thank you for polishing my words and making them sing.

To my designer, Jan Westendorp, you inspire me with your can-do attitude and your creative design skills. It is delightful working with you.

To the team at Printing Legacy, you put the icing on the cake.

To my Kitchen Cabinet, my closest advisors, you know who you are, and I value and treasure each and every one of you for your wisdom and counsel: Judy, Karin, Wendy, Toby, Jody, Eleanor, Marlene (both of you), Alison and, most of all, Joel

Rosenberg. Without your love, understanding, patience and sense of humour, none of this would be possible.

To my family . . . all of you wonderful human beings inspire me to be better and I am so grateful you are mine.

About the Author

What I Wish I'd Said: And Other Things that Keep Me Up at Night is Marjie Zacks' third book. Her first two books, *It All Ends Up in a Parfait Glass: A Tribute to My Mother's Wisdom* and *Tales from The Curio Cabinet* have delighted readers with stories of family, foibles, and the indignities and wisdom of aging. Originally from Peterborough and Ottawa, Ontario, Marjie has an M.A. in Education and has spent thirty-eight years in public relations. Writing is her second career, and she is also a popular public speaker. Marjie lives in the Toronto area where she spends her time with her adored husband and adoring soft coated wheaten terrier, Winnie. She is Bubbie to three wonderful grandkids.

www.ingramcontent.com/pod-product-compliance
Lightning Source LLC
Chambersburg PA
CBHW060359080526
44583CB00012B/382